Katoomba:
Blue Mountains Vistas

Katoomba:
Blue Mountains Vistas

Rob Benton

Esotericom®

All photographs by Rob Benton

ISBN 978-0-9980682-6-8

He covers the heavens with clouds,

He prepares rain for the earth,

He makes grass grow upon the hills.

Psalms 147: 8

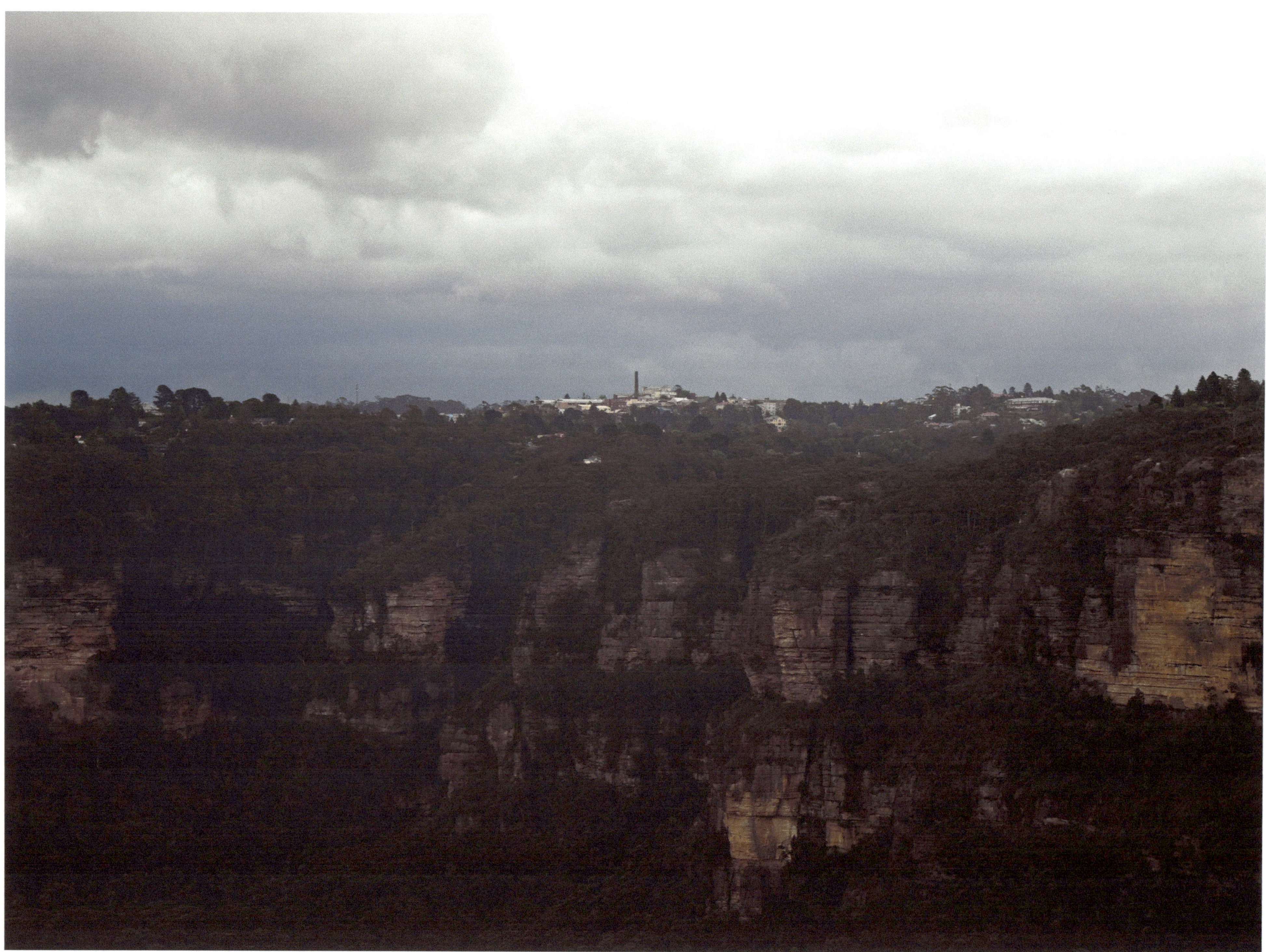

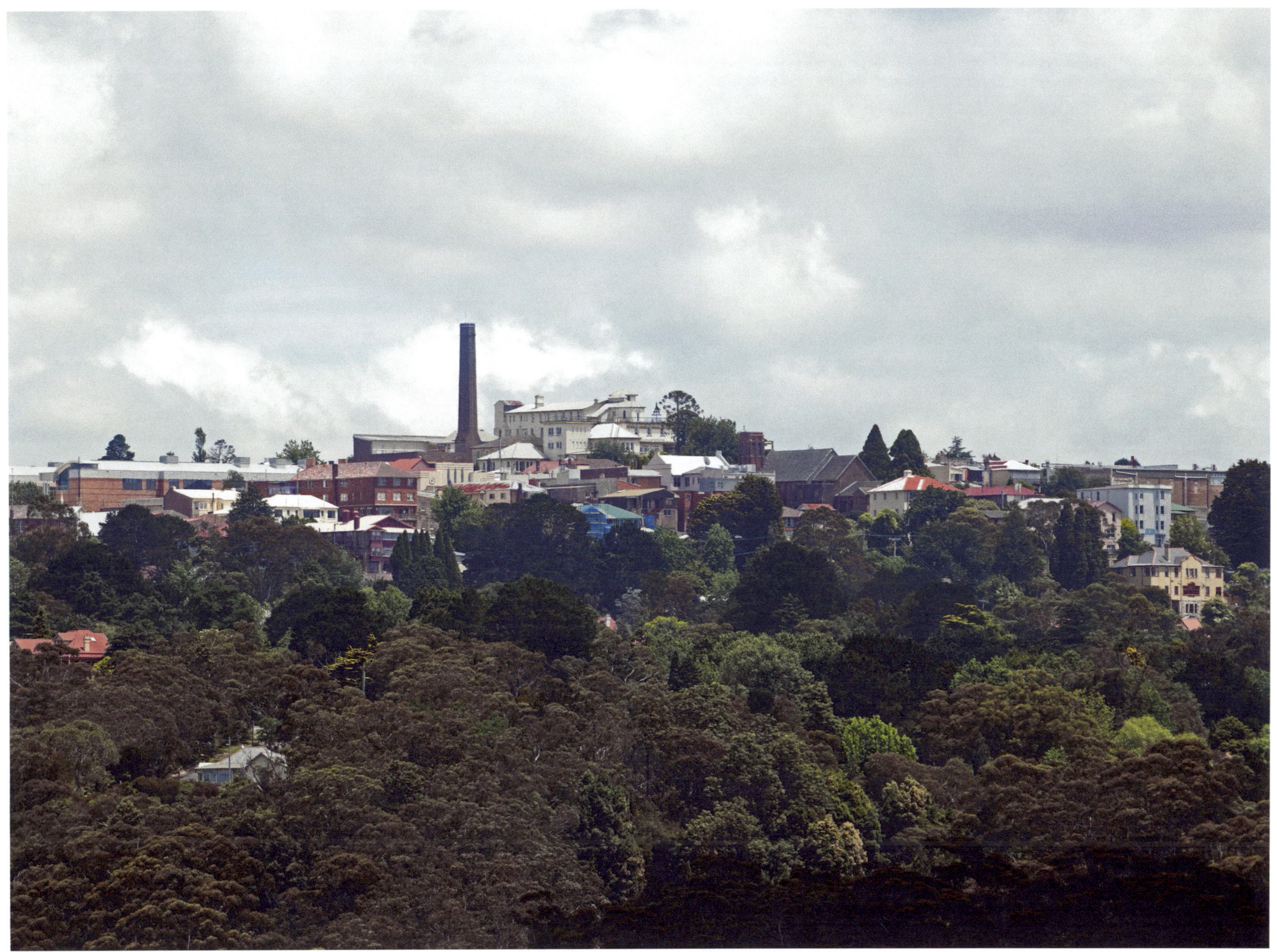

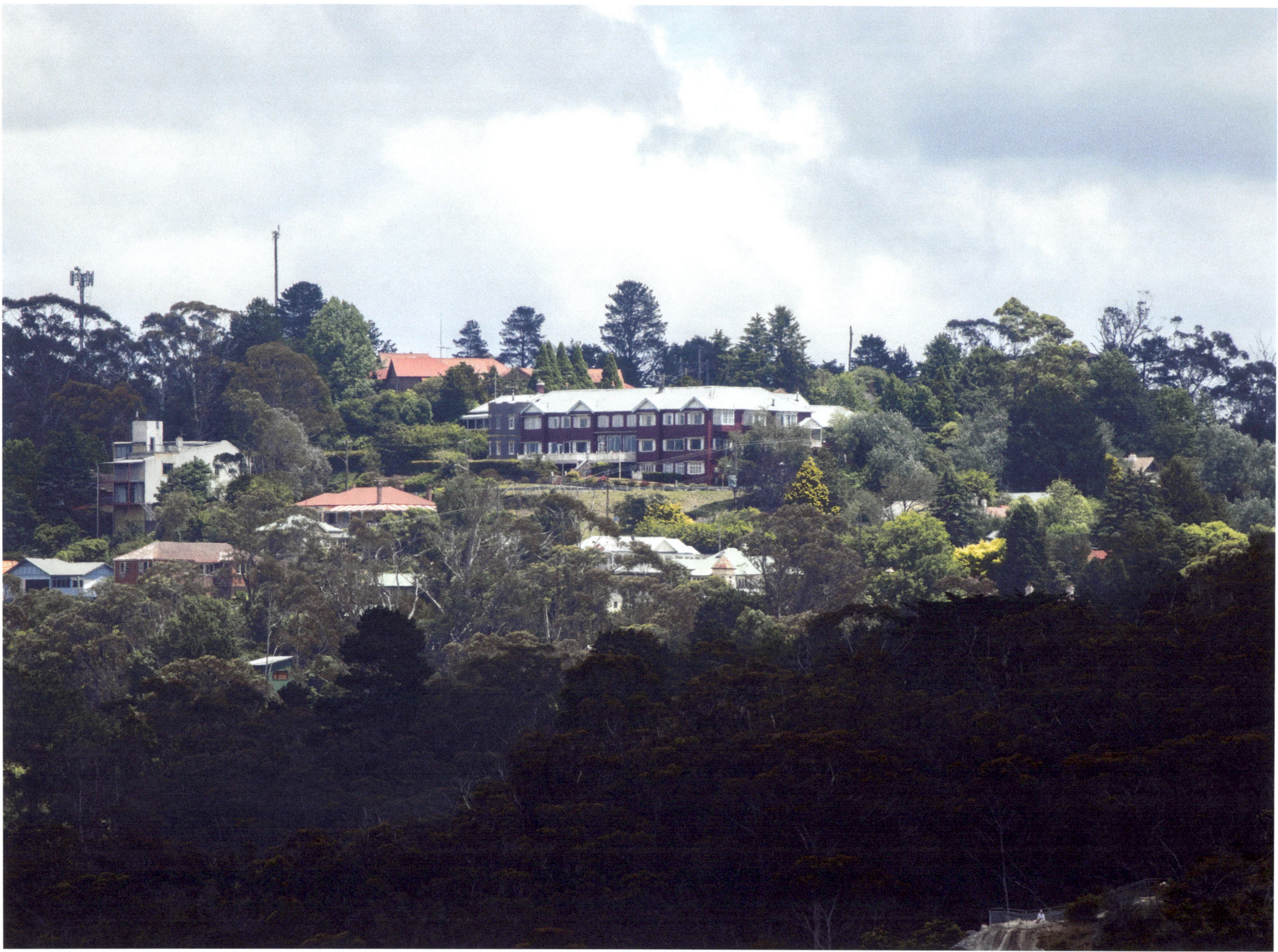

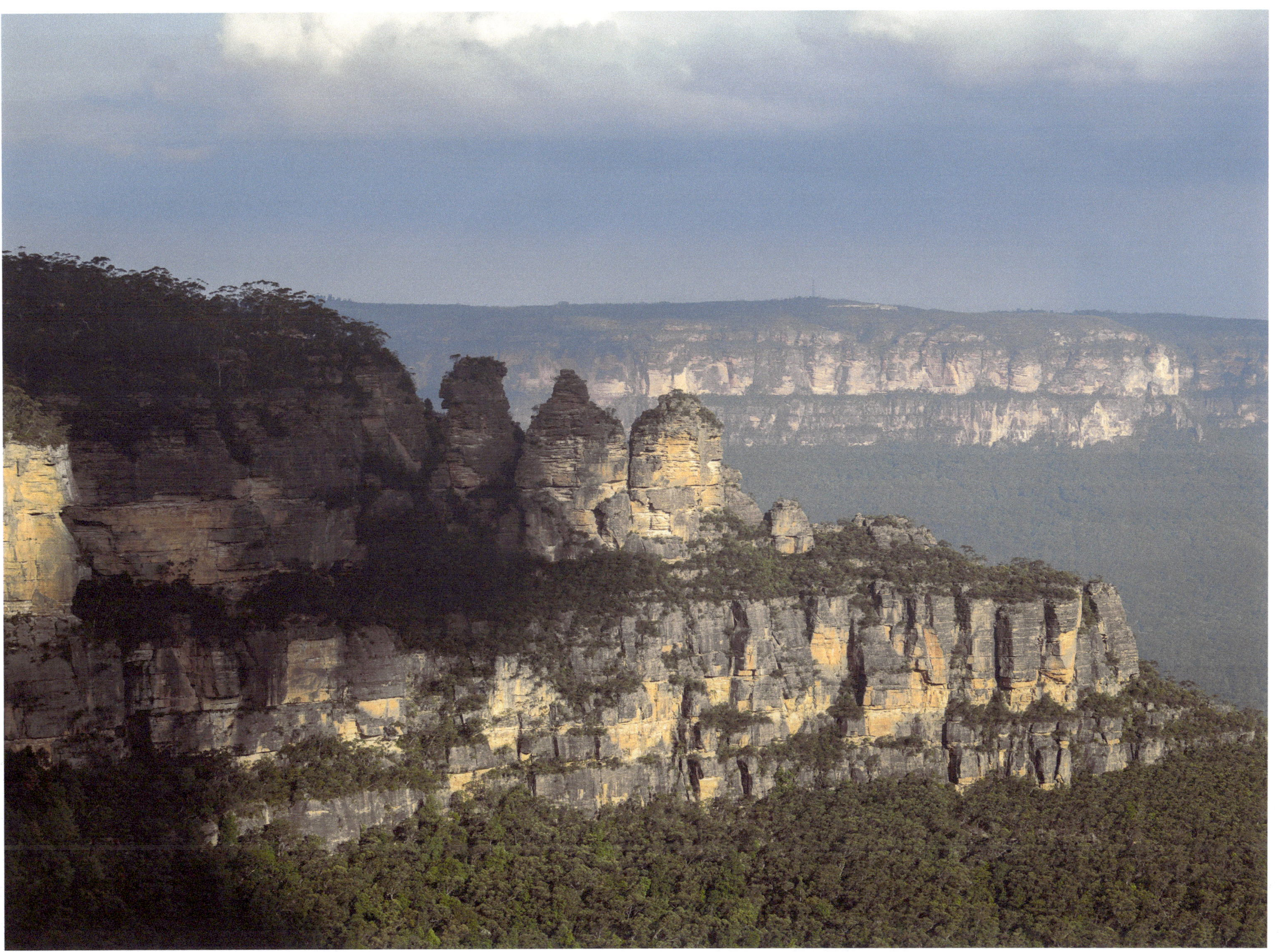

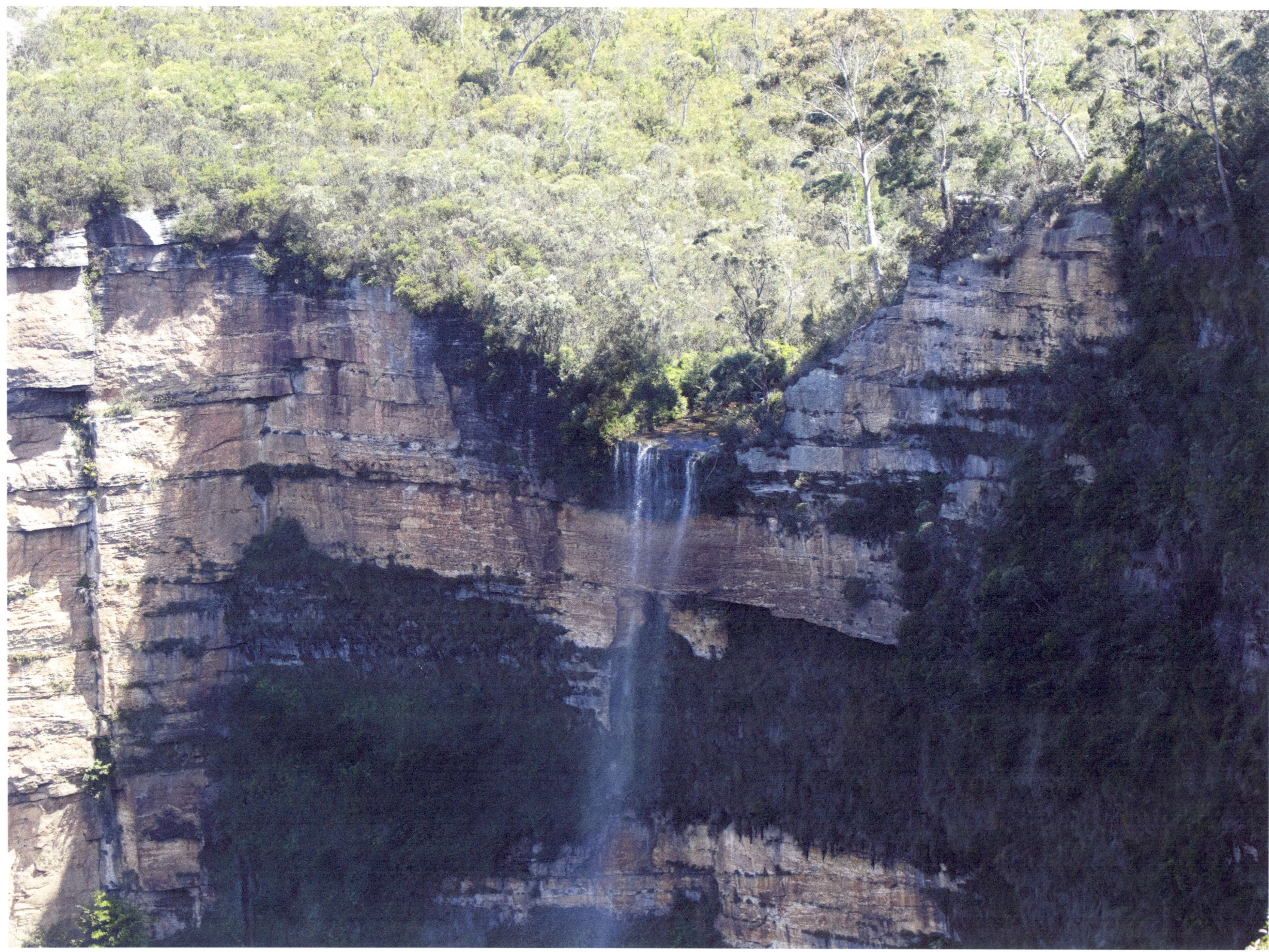

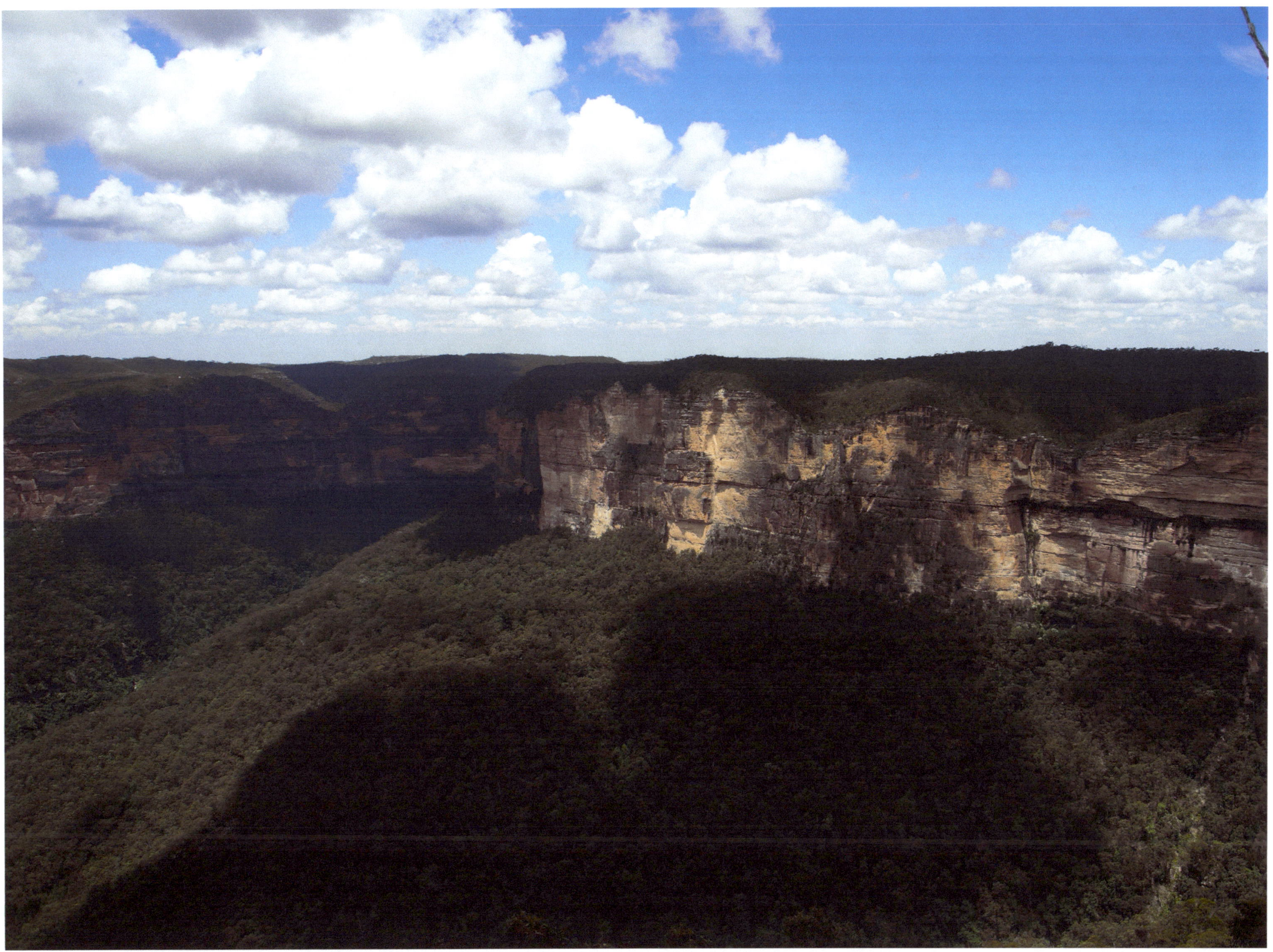

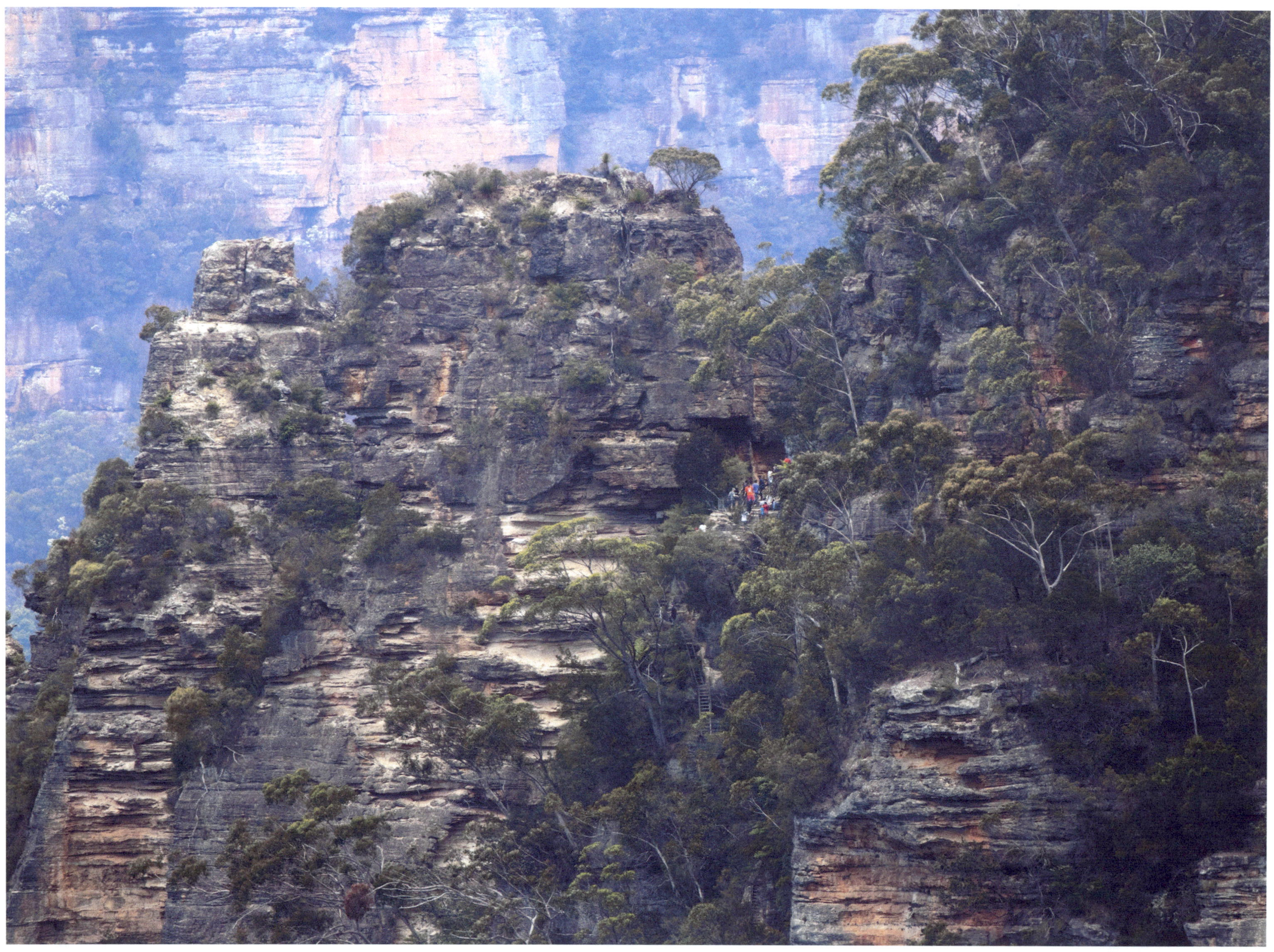

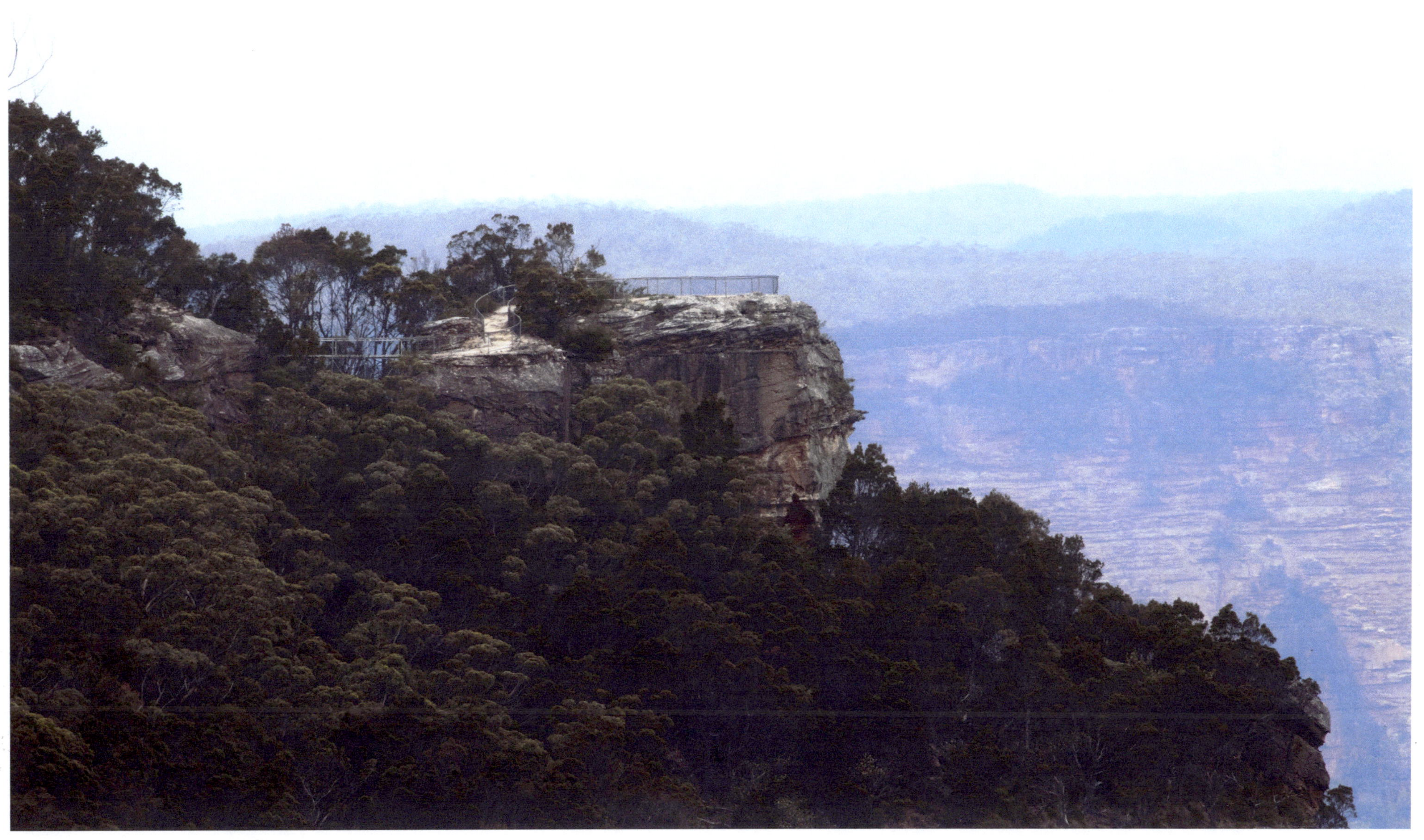

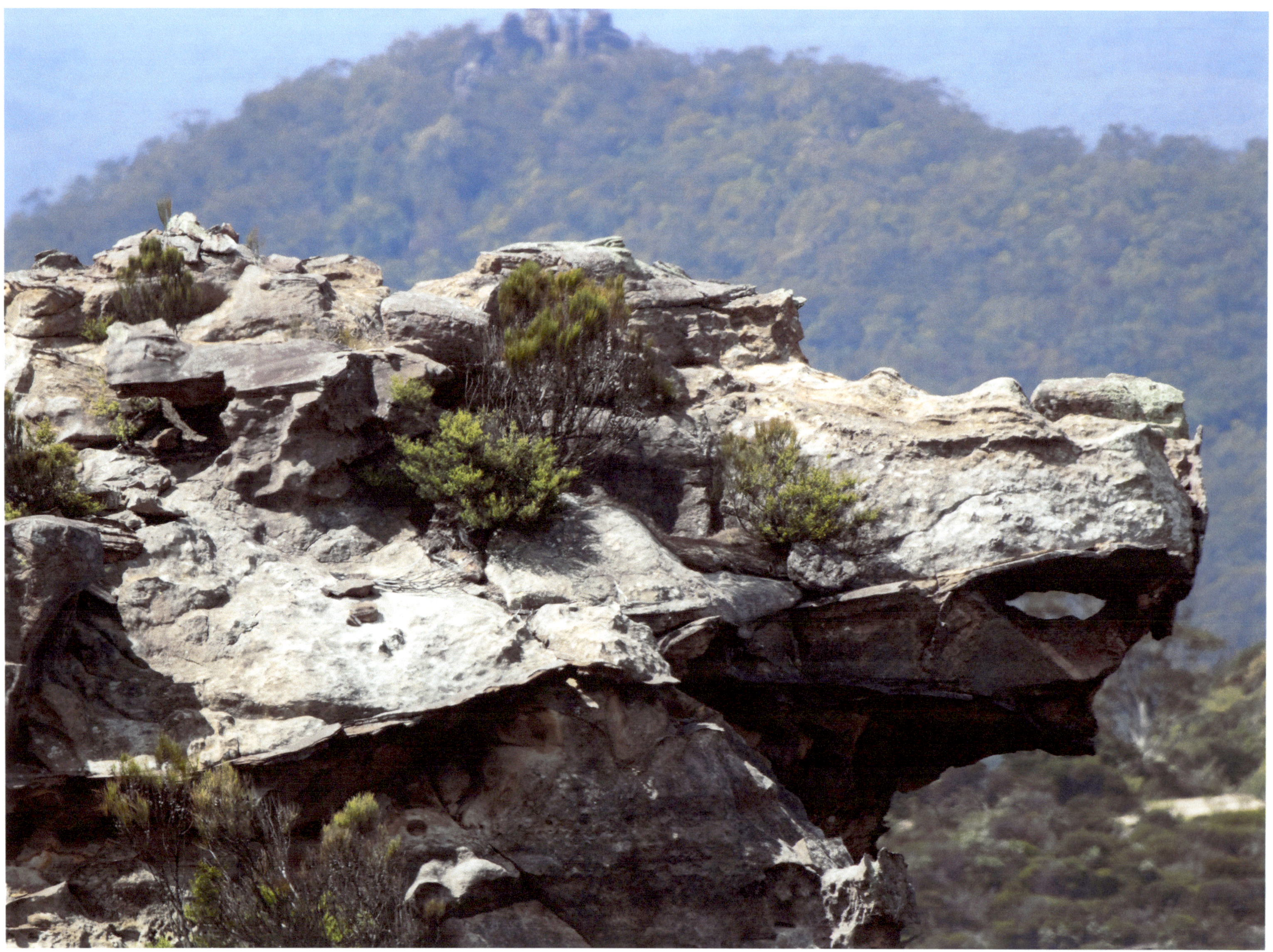

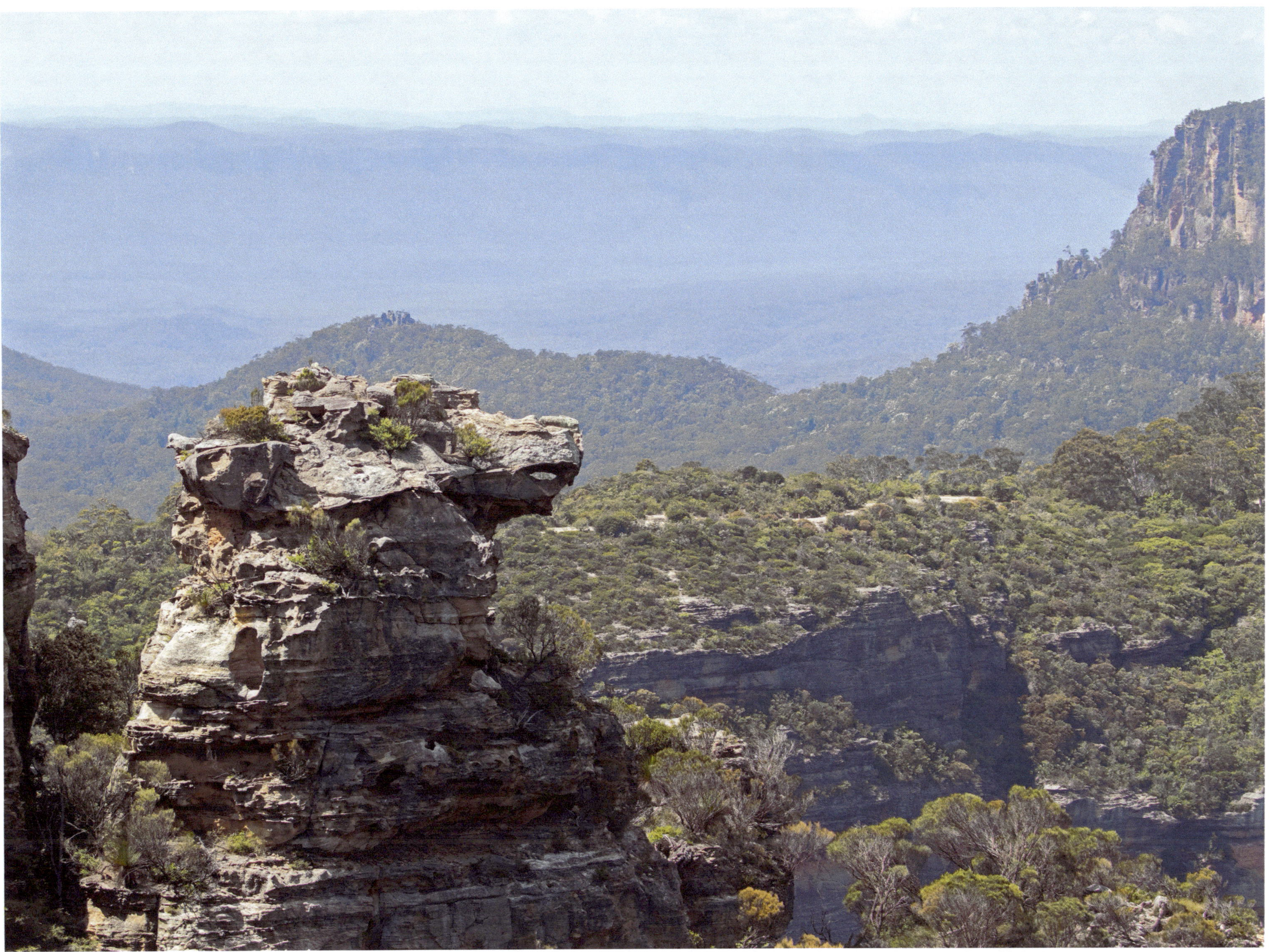

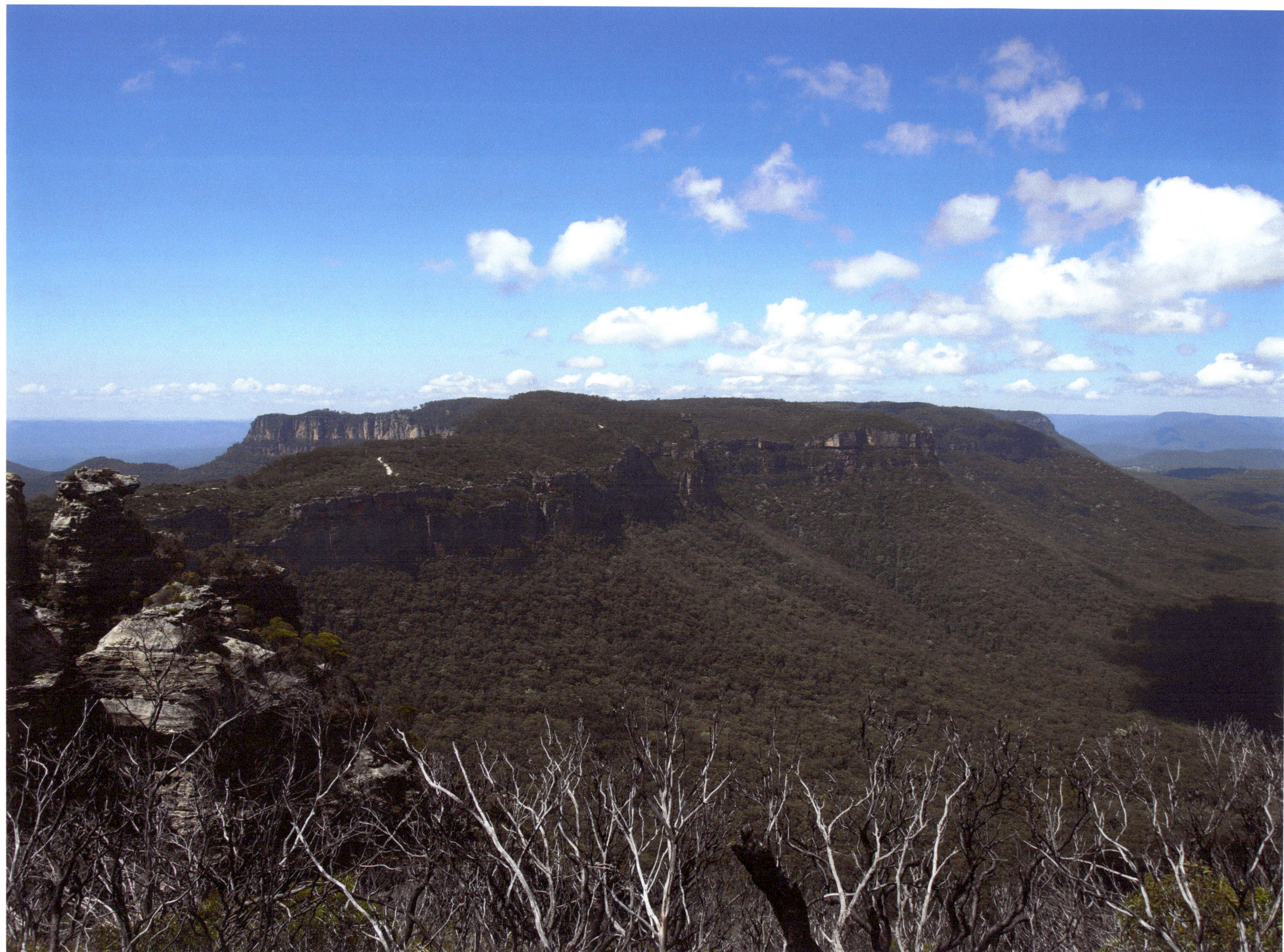

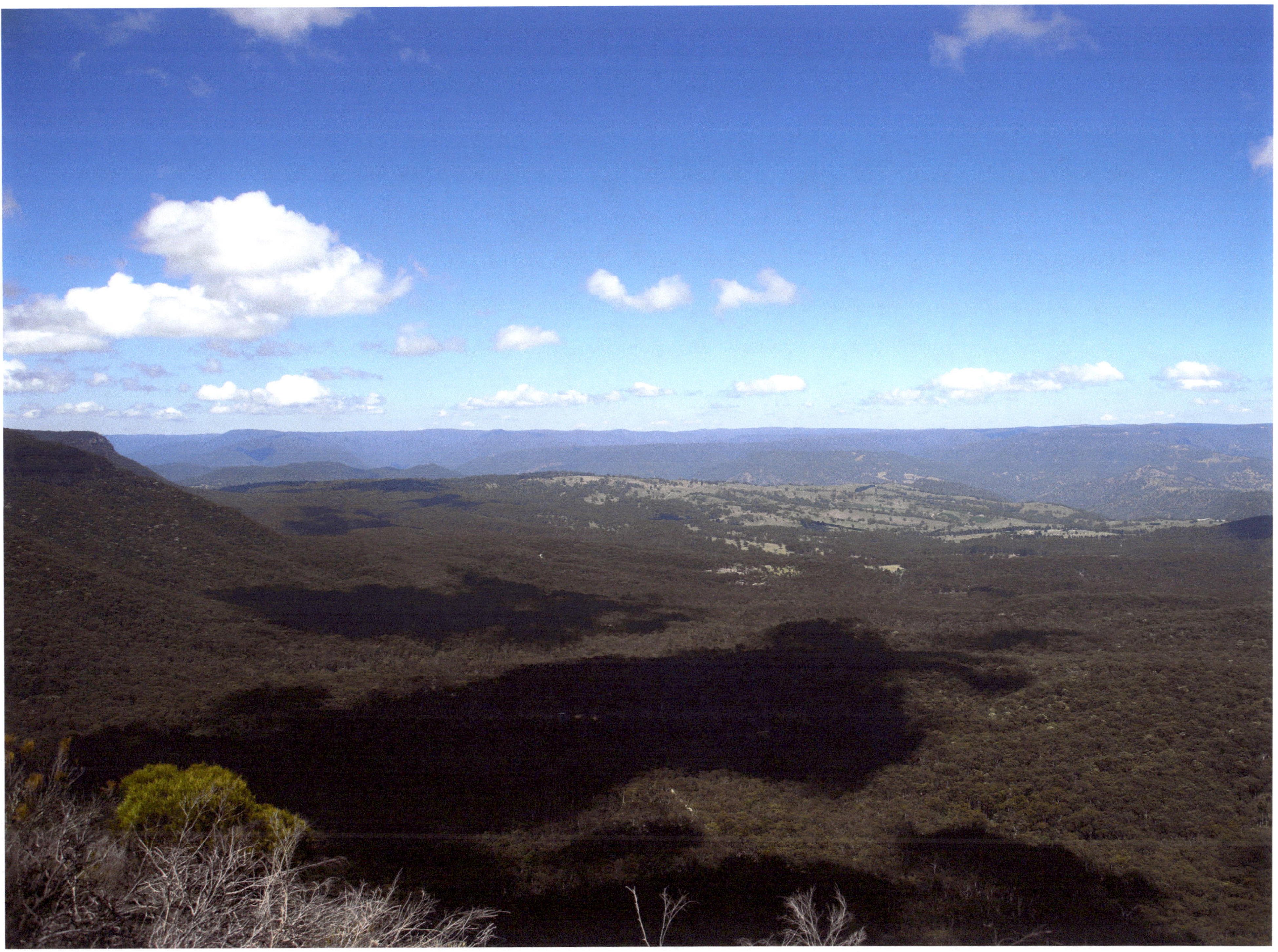

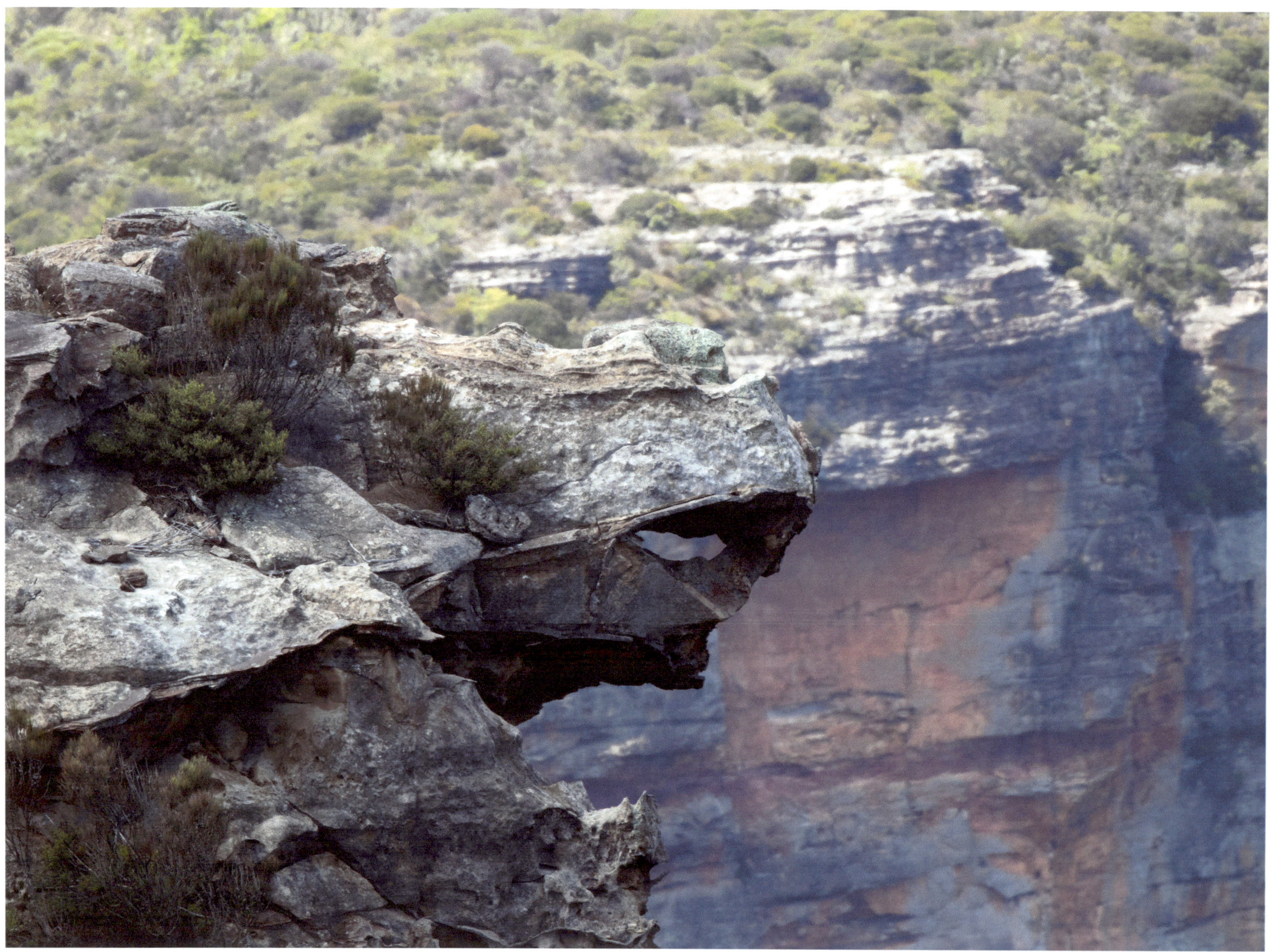

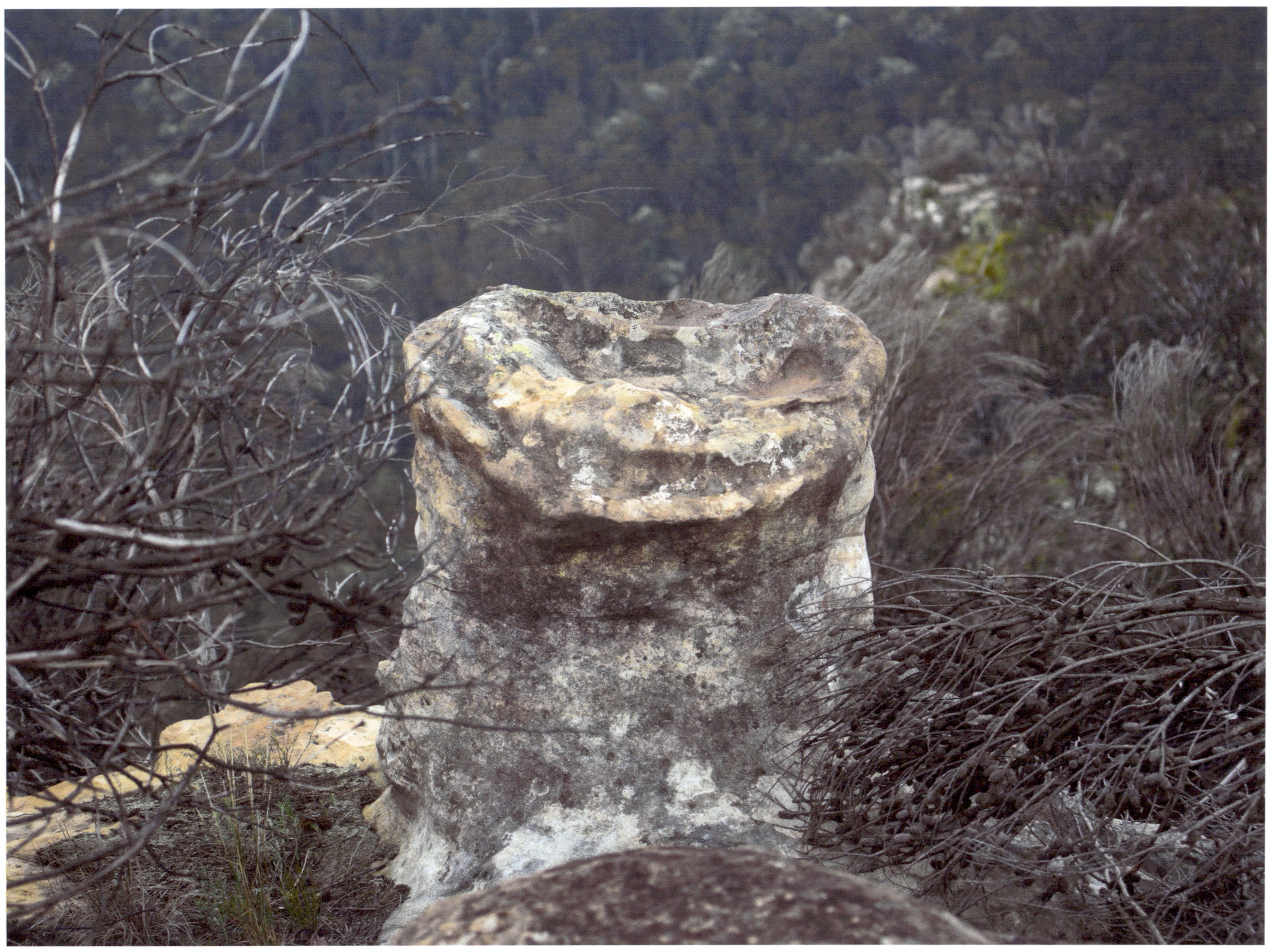

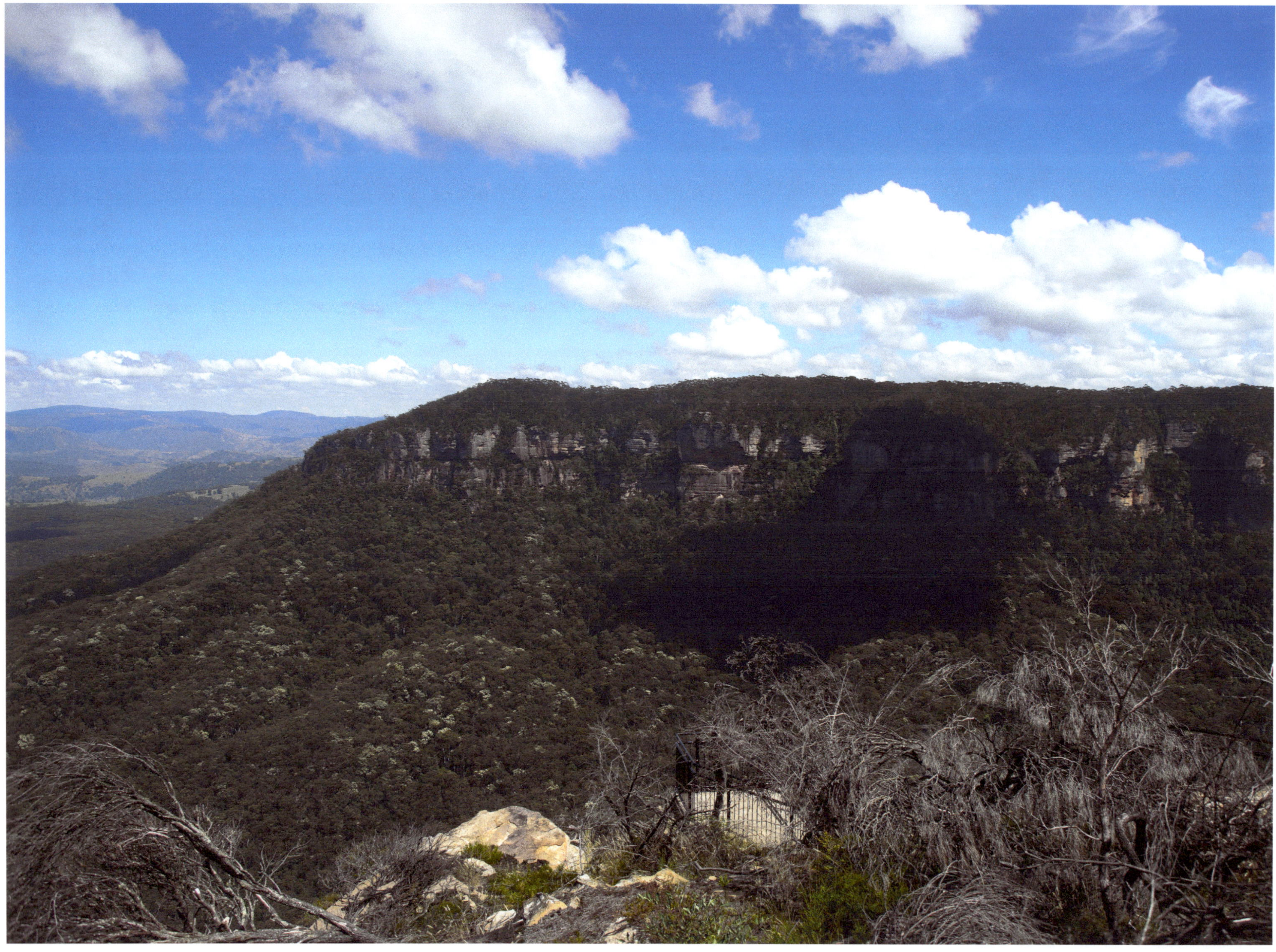

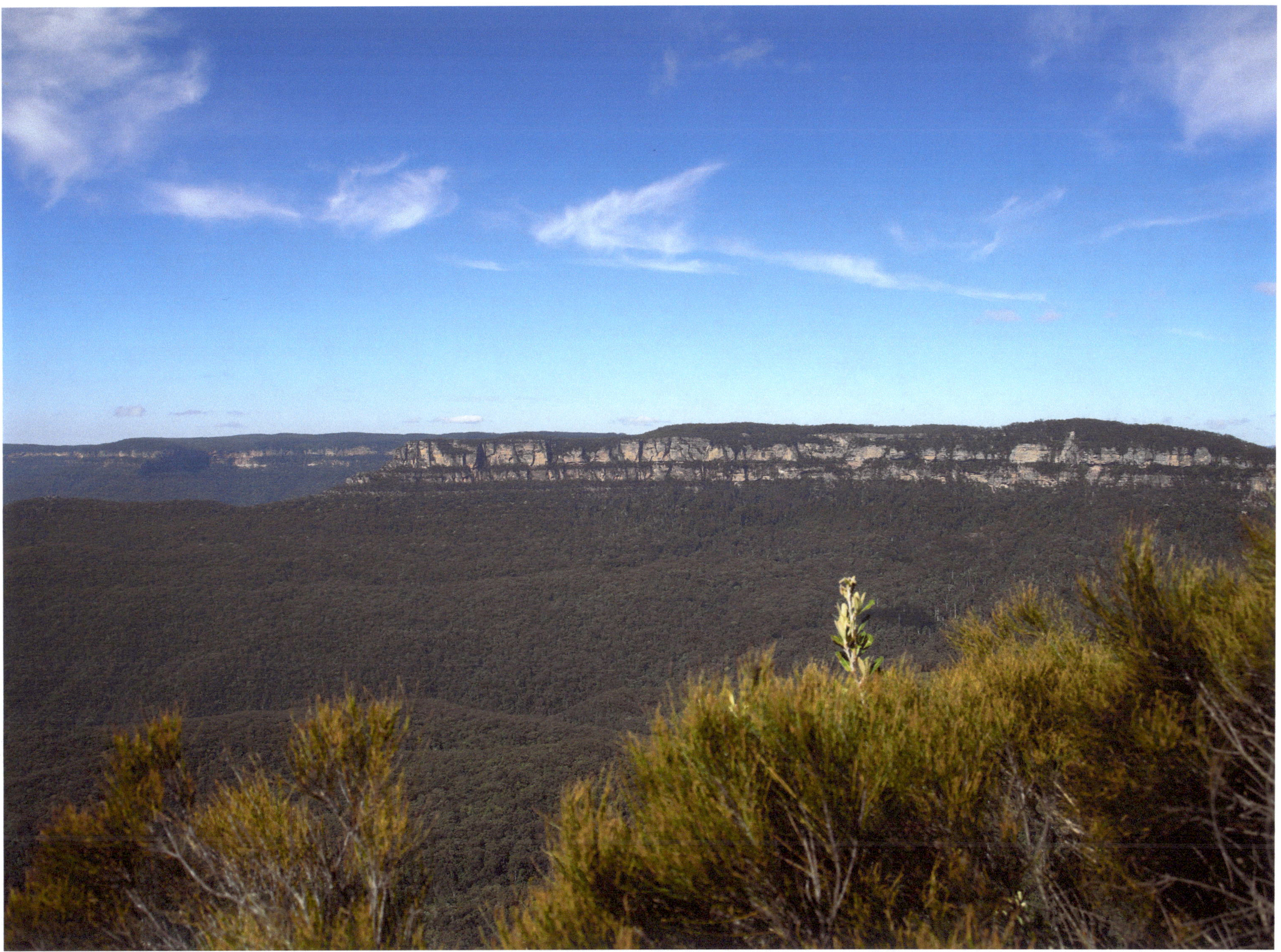

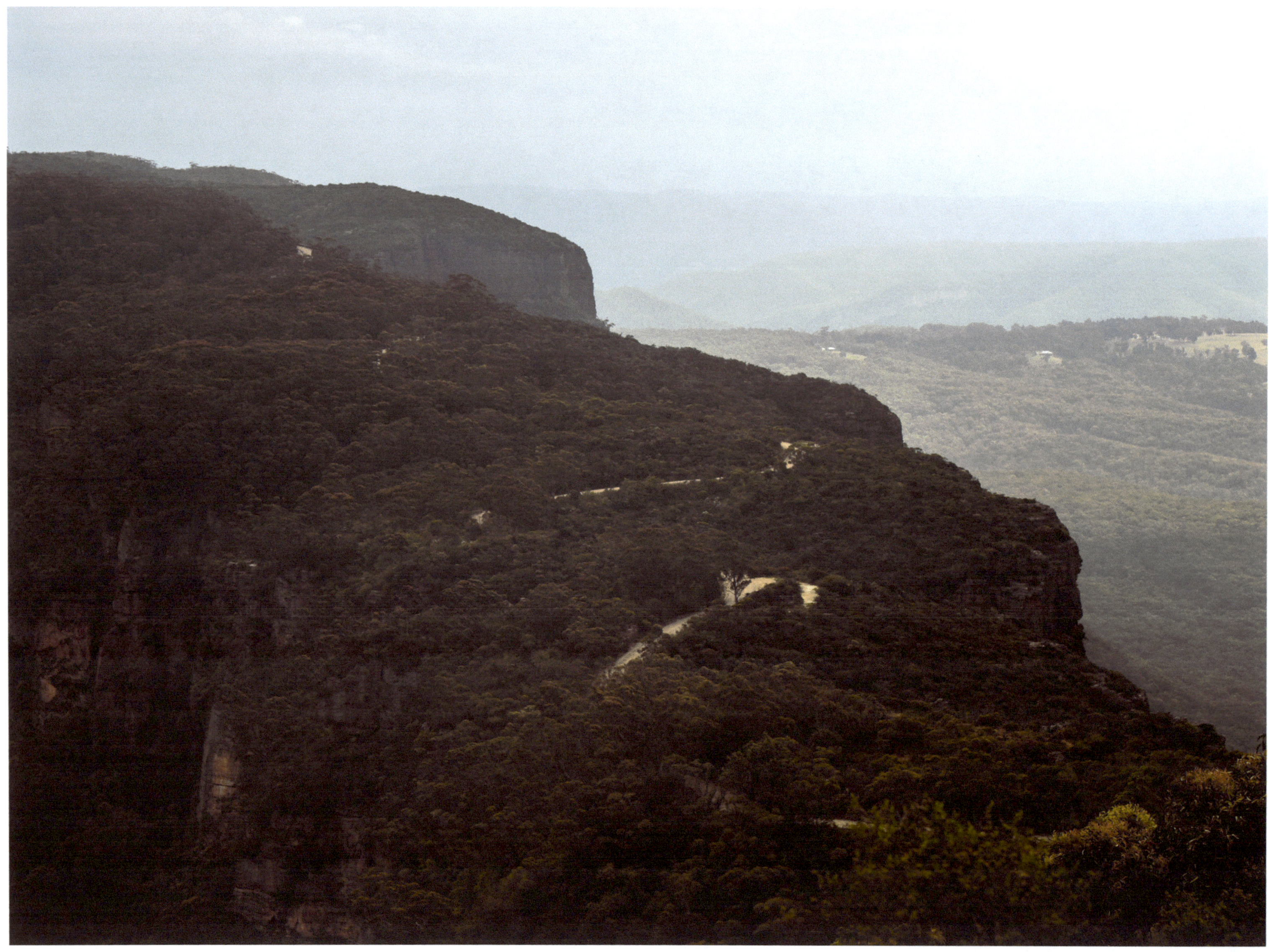

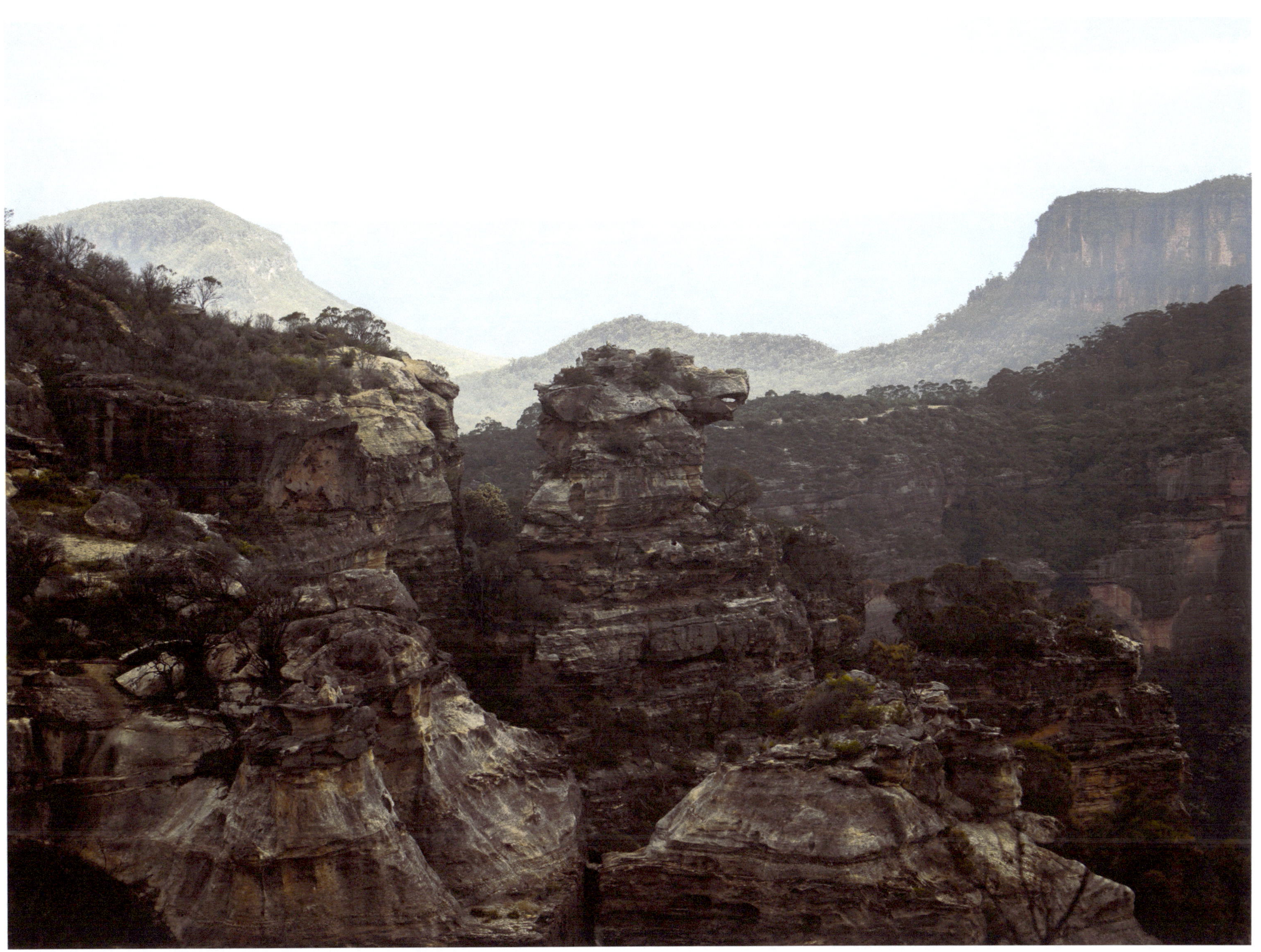

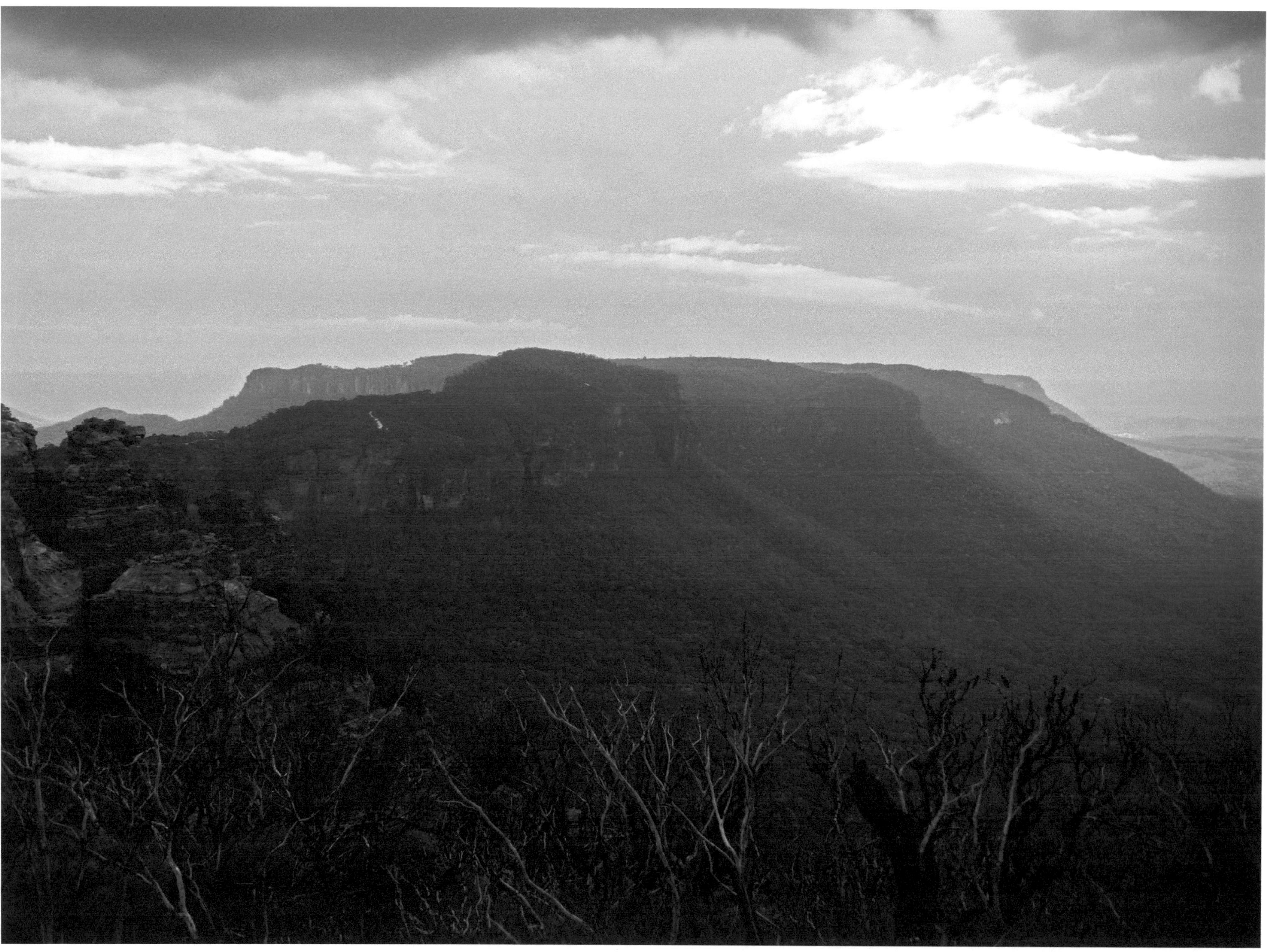

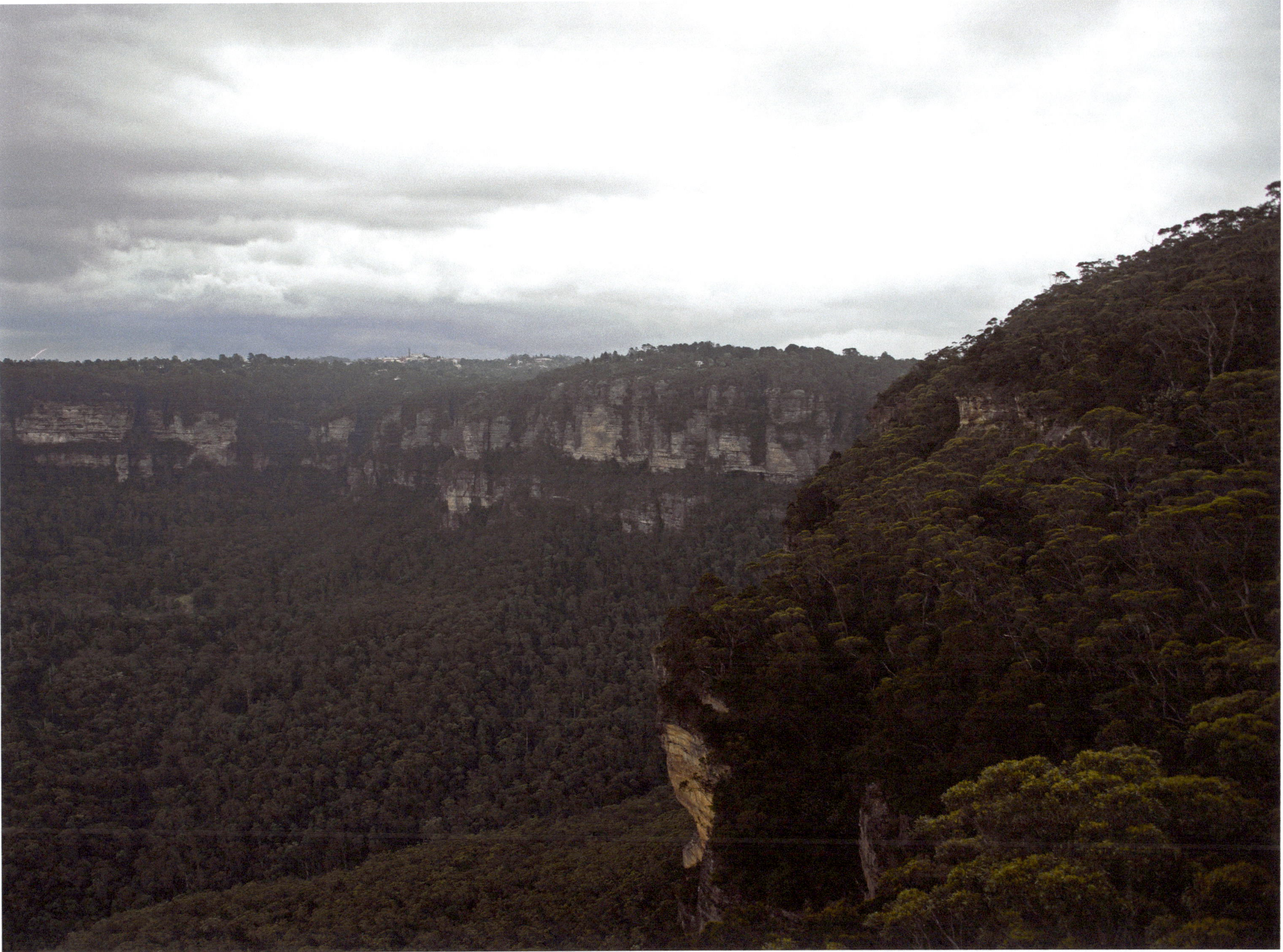

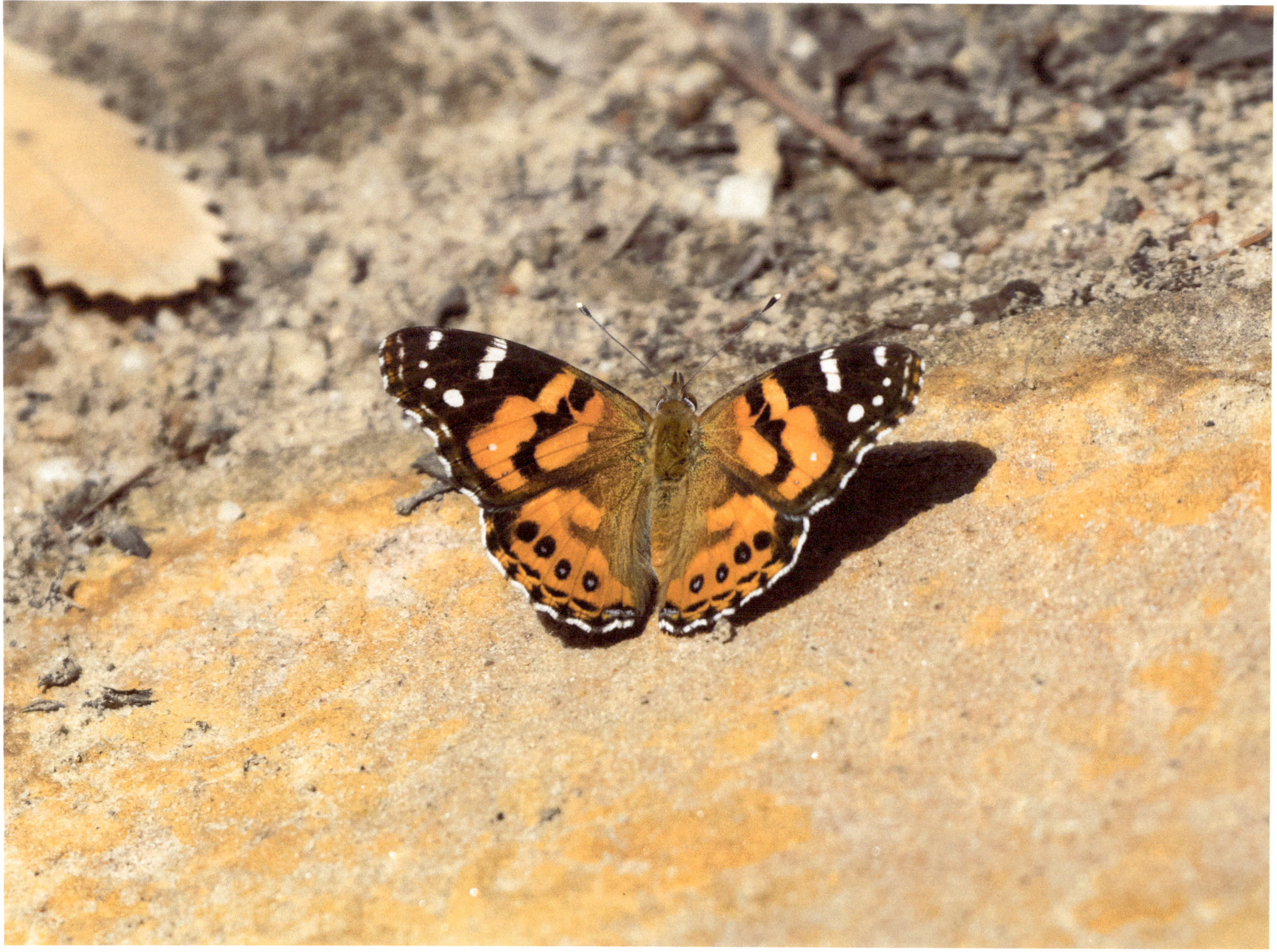

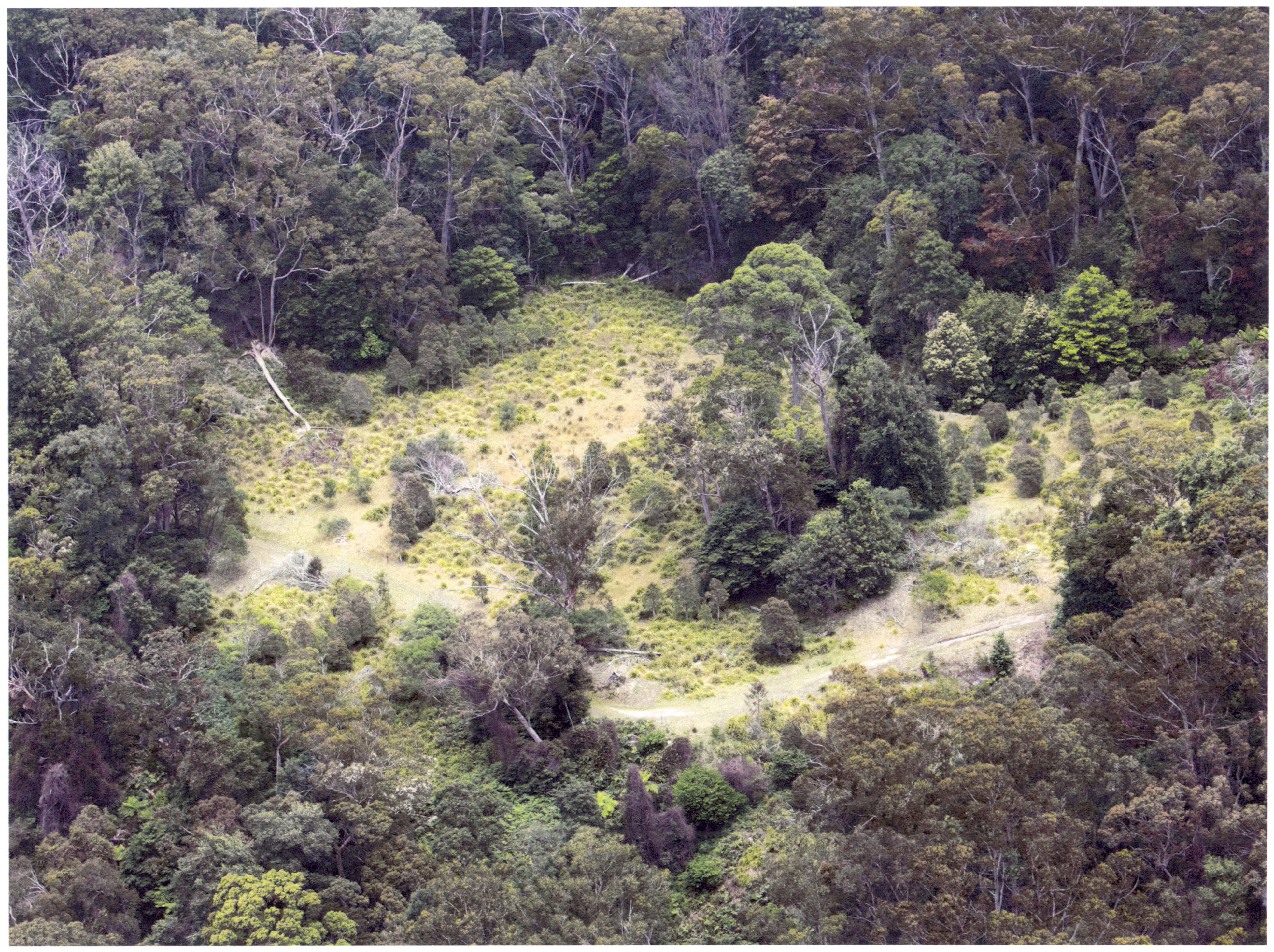

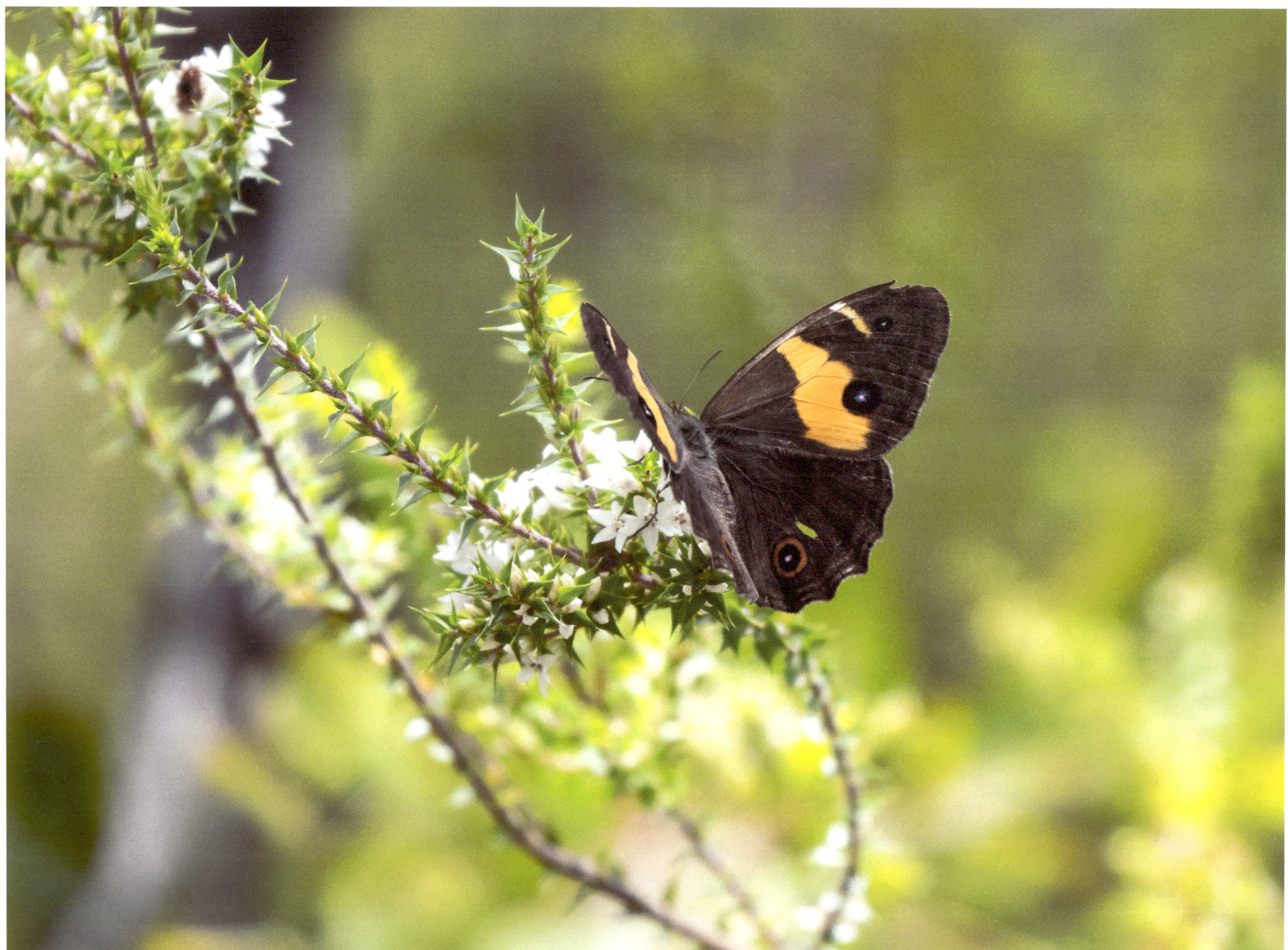

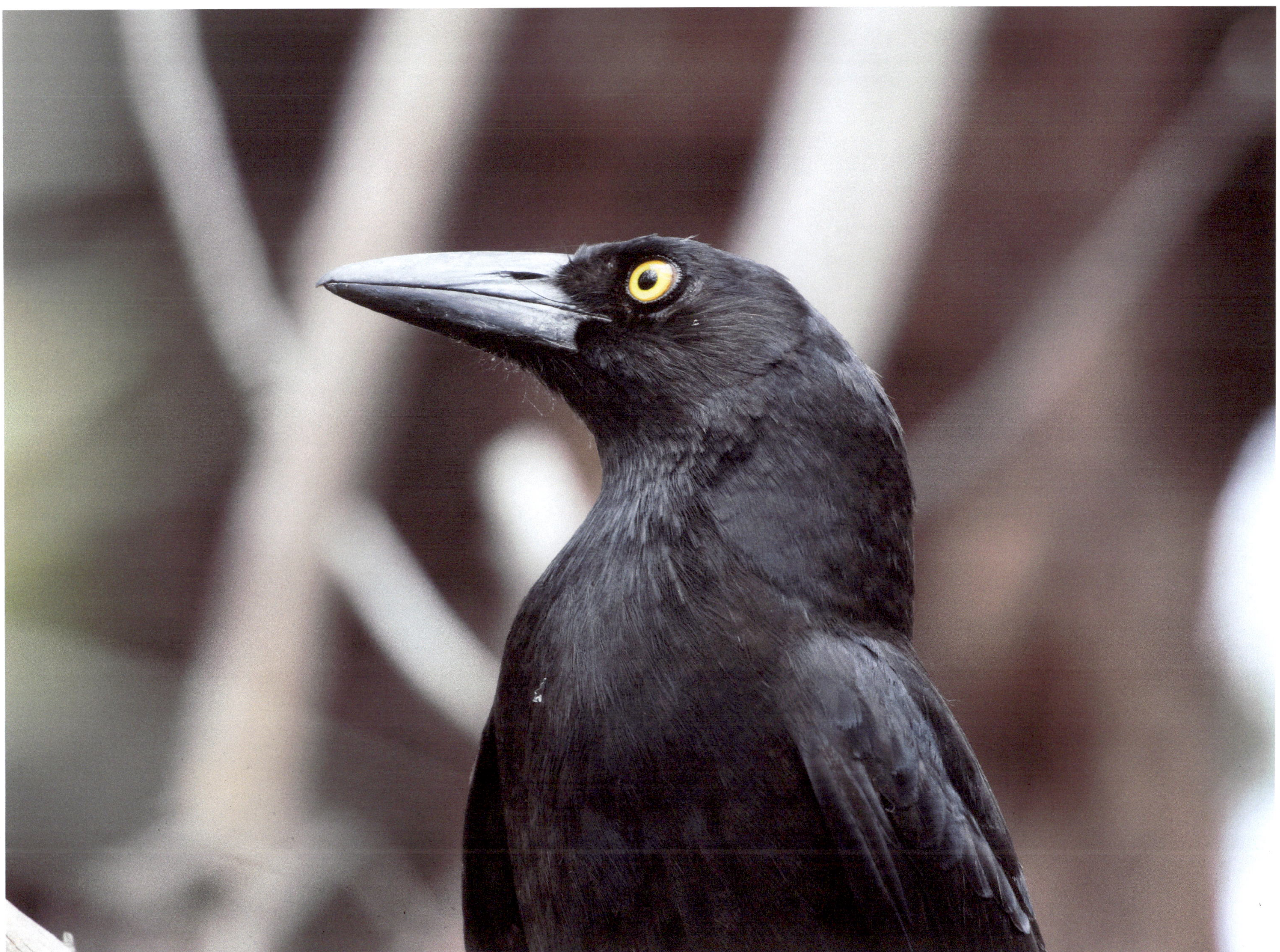

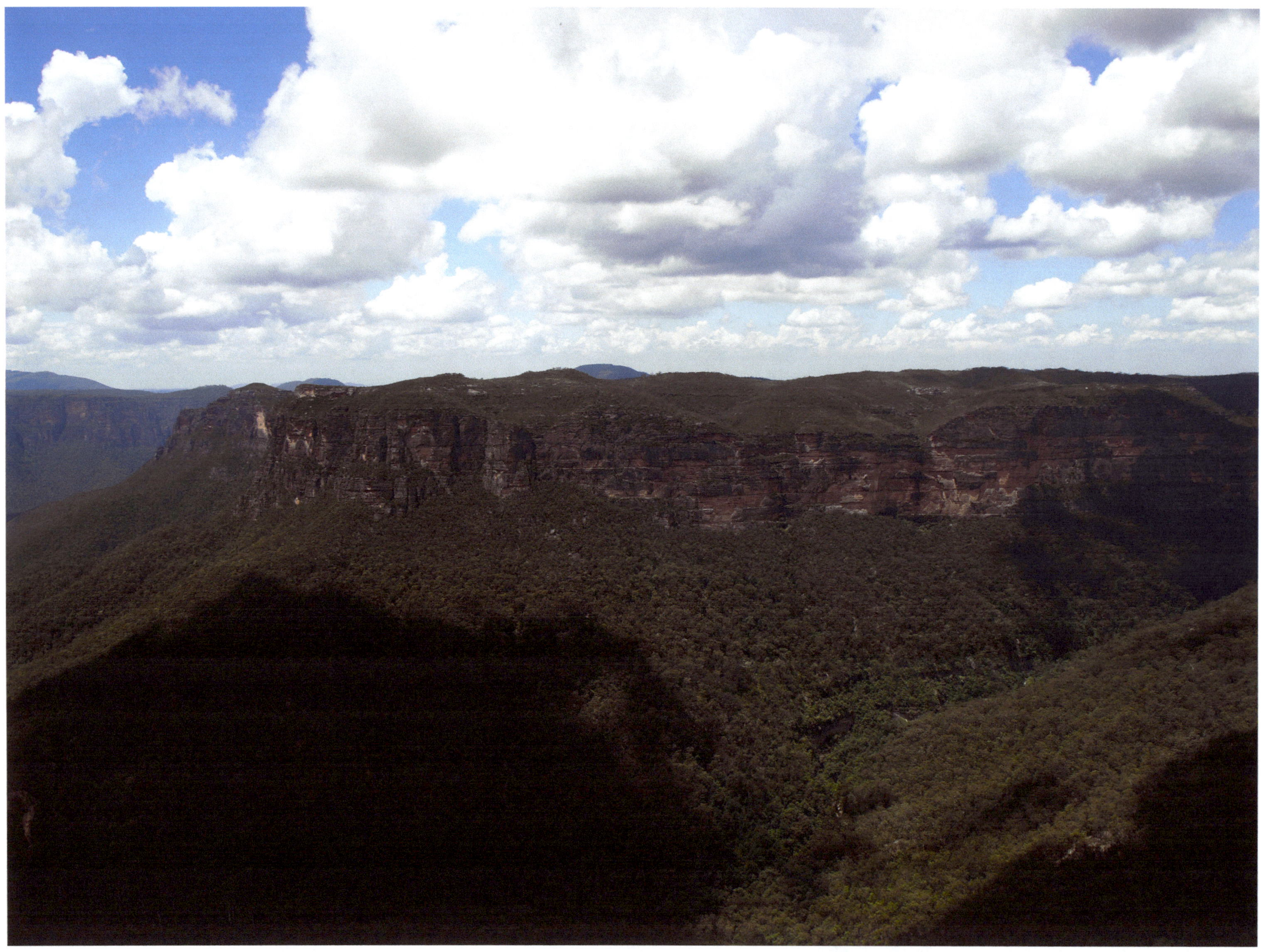

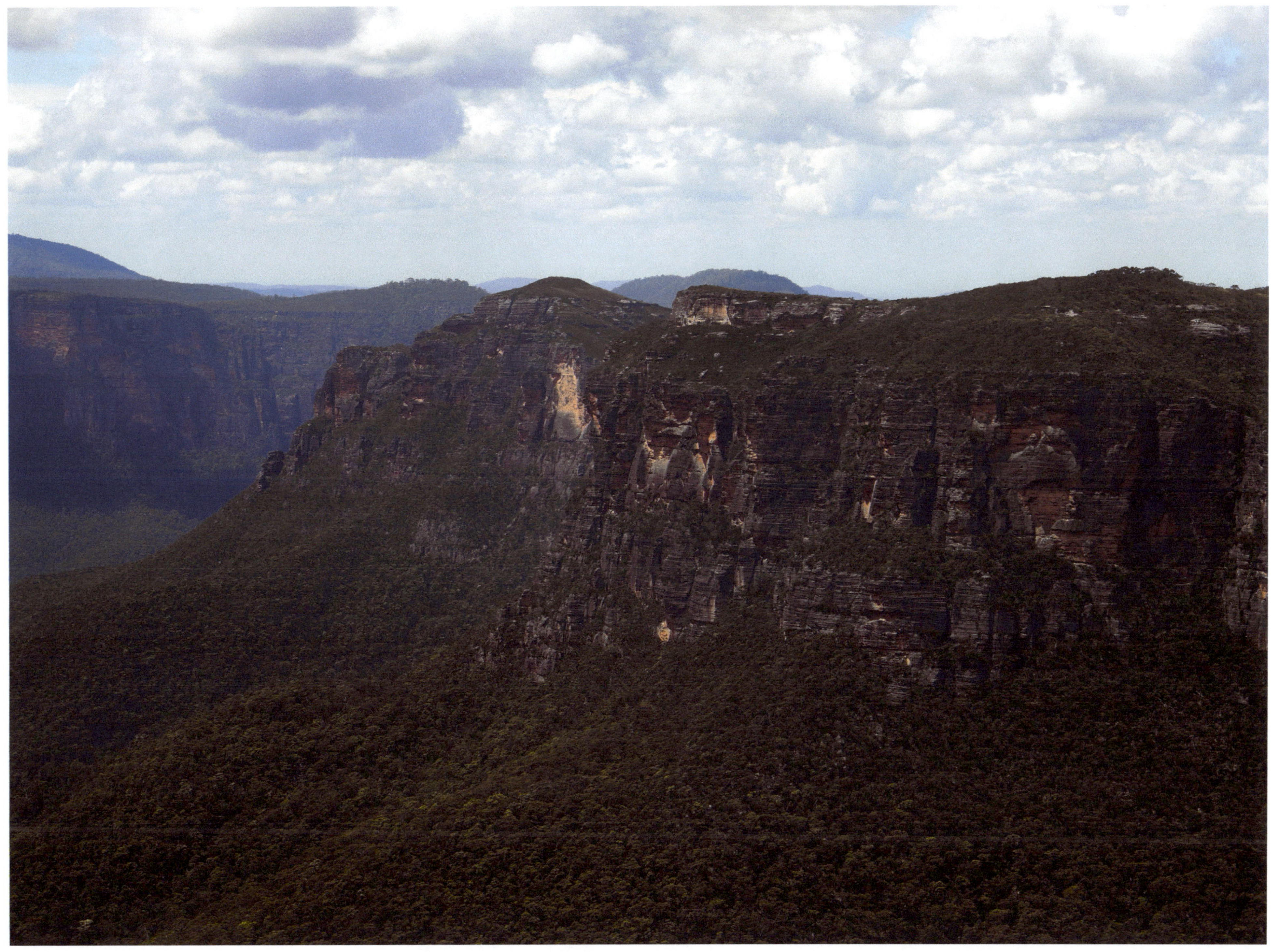

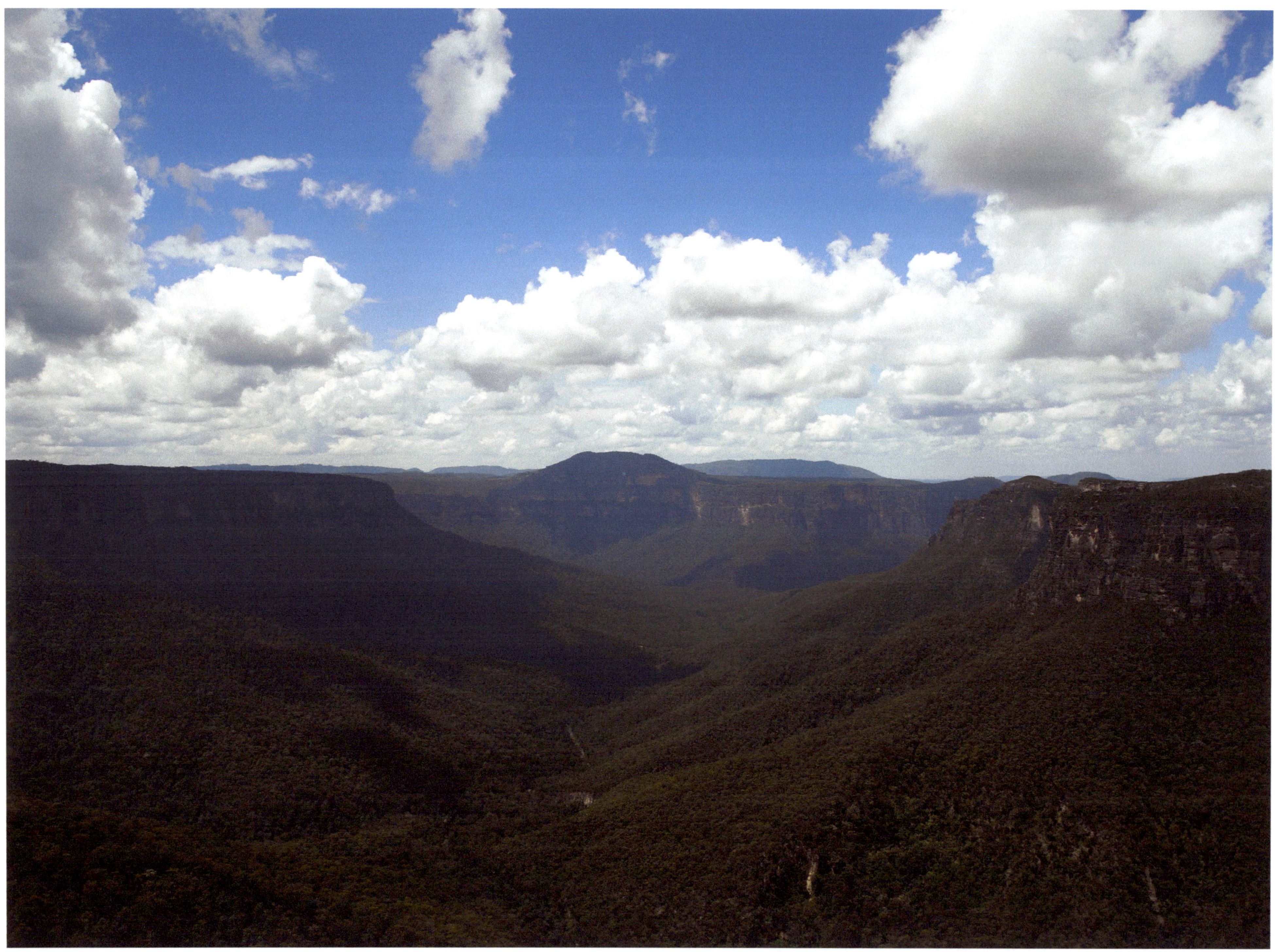

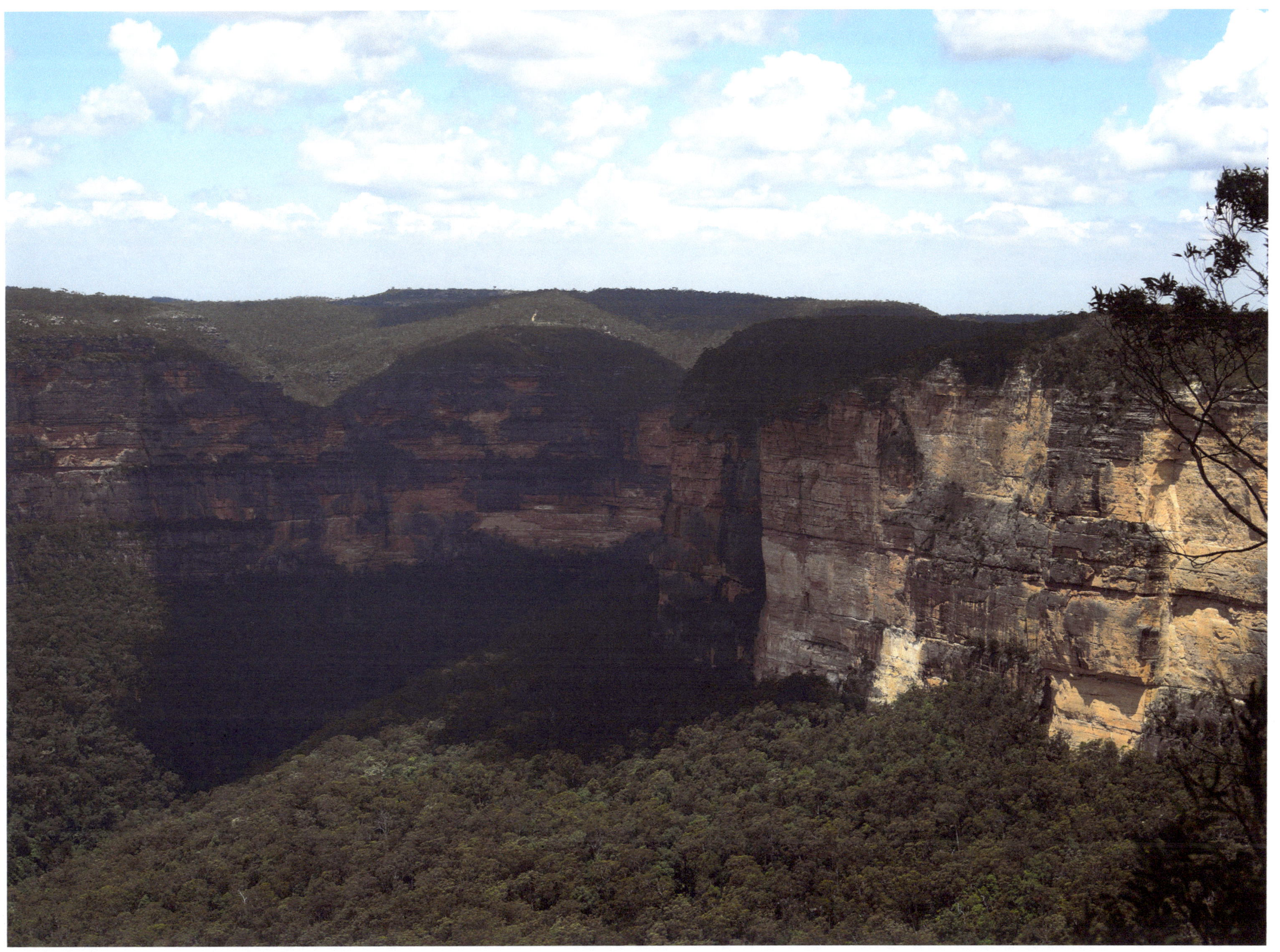

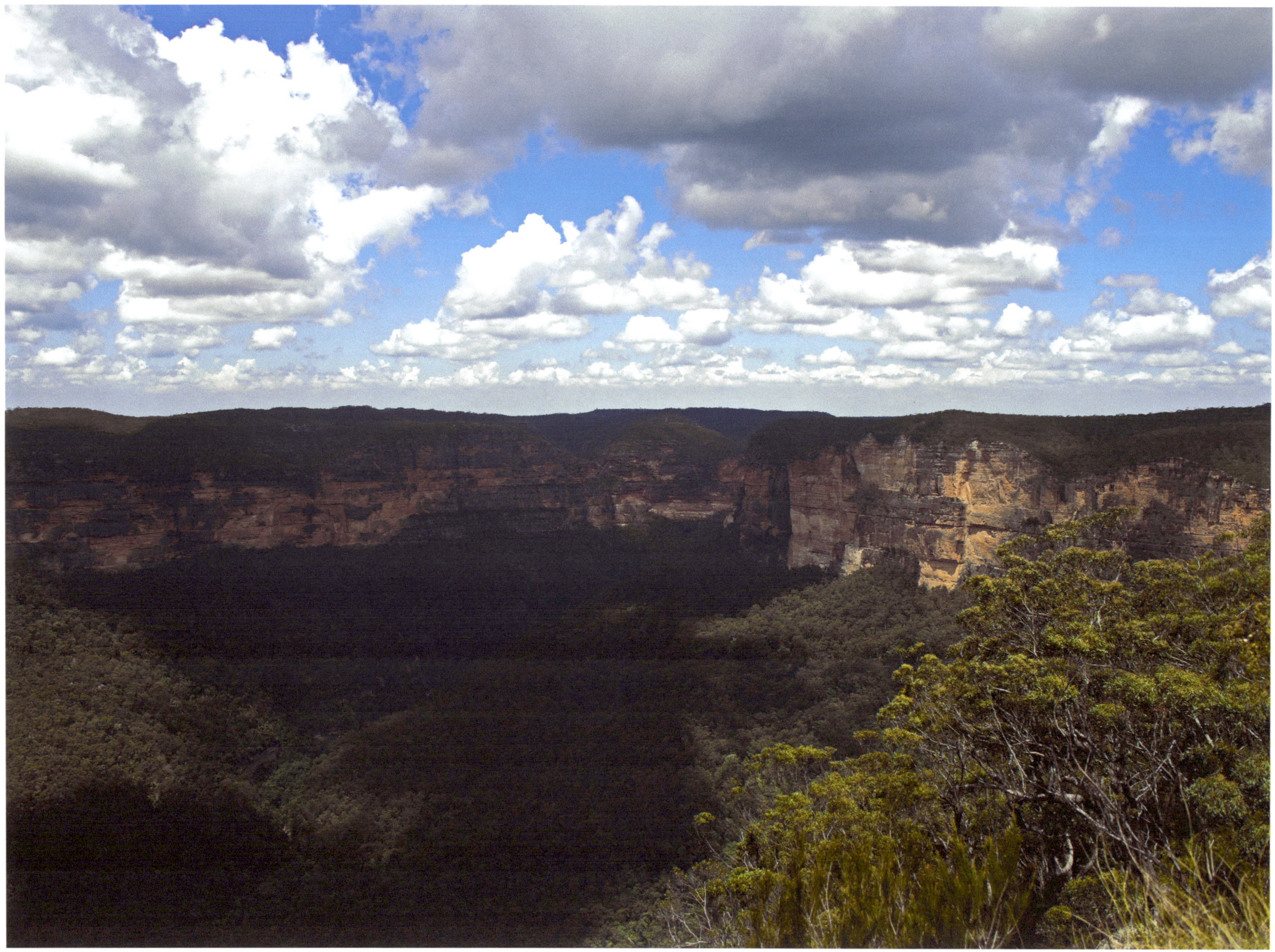

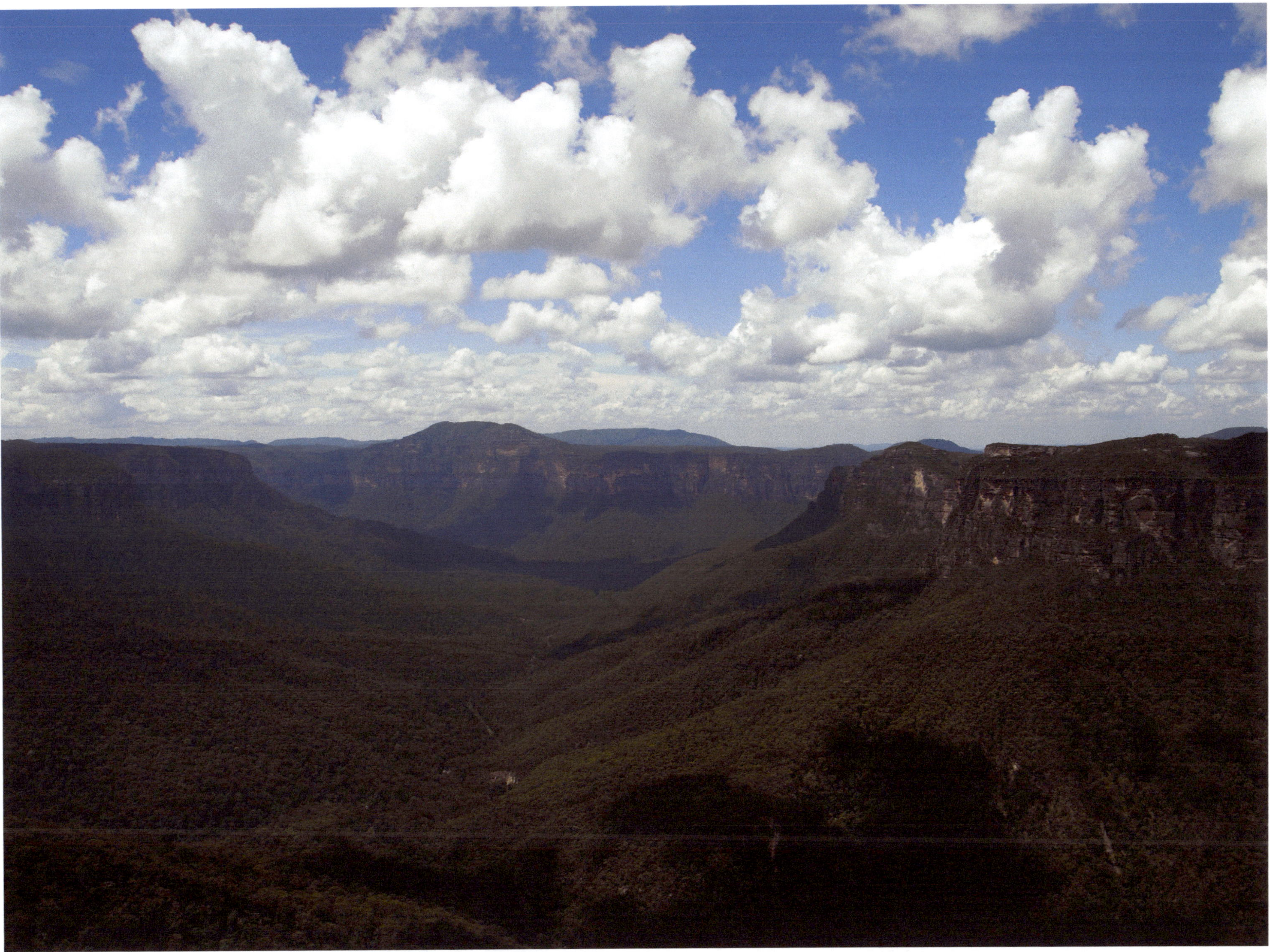

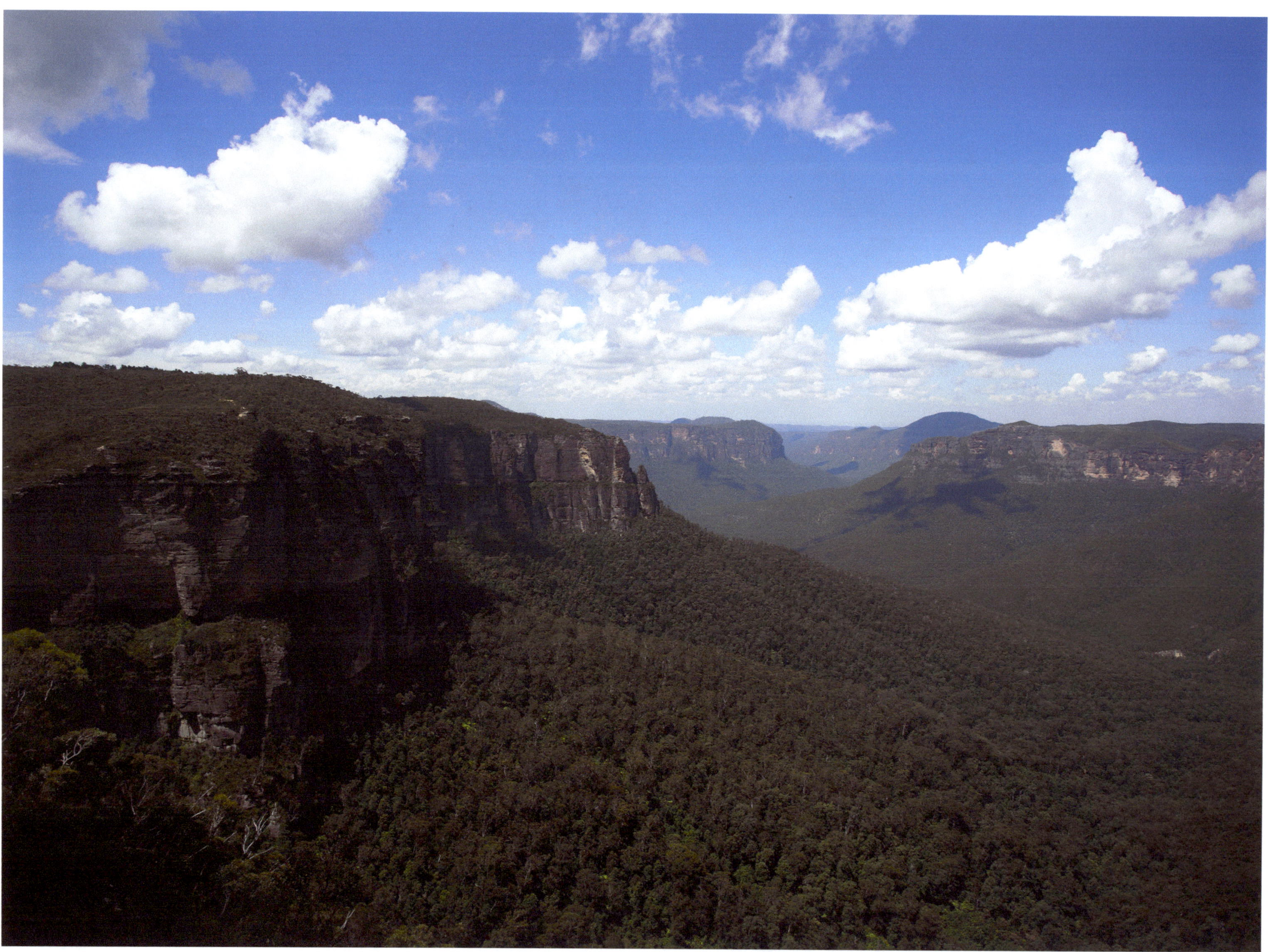

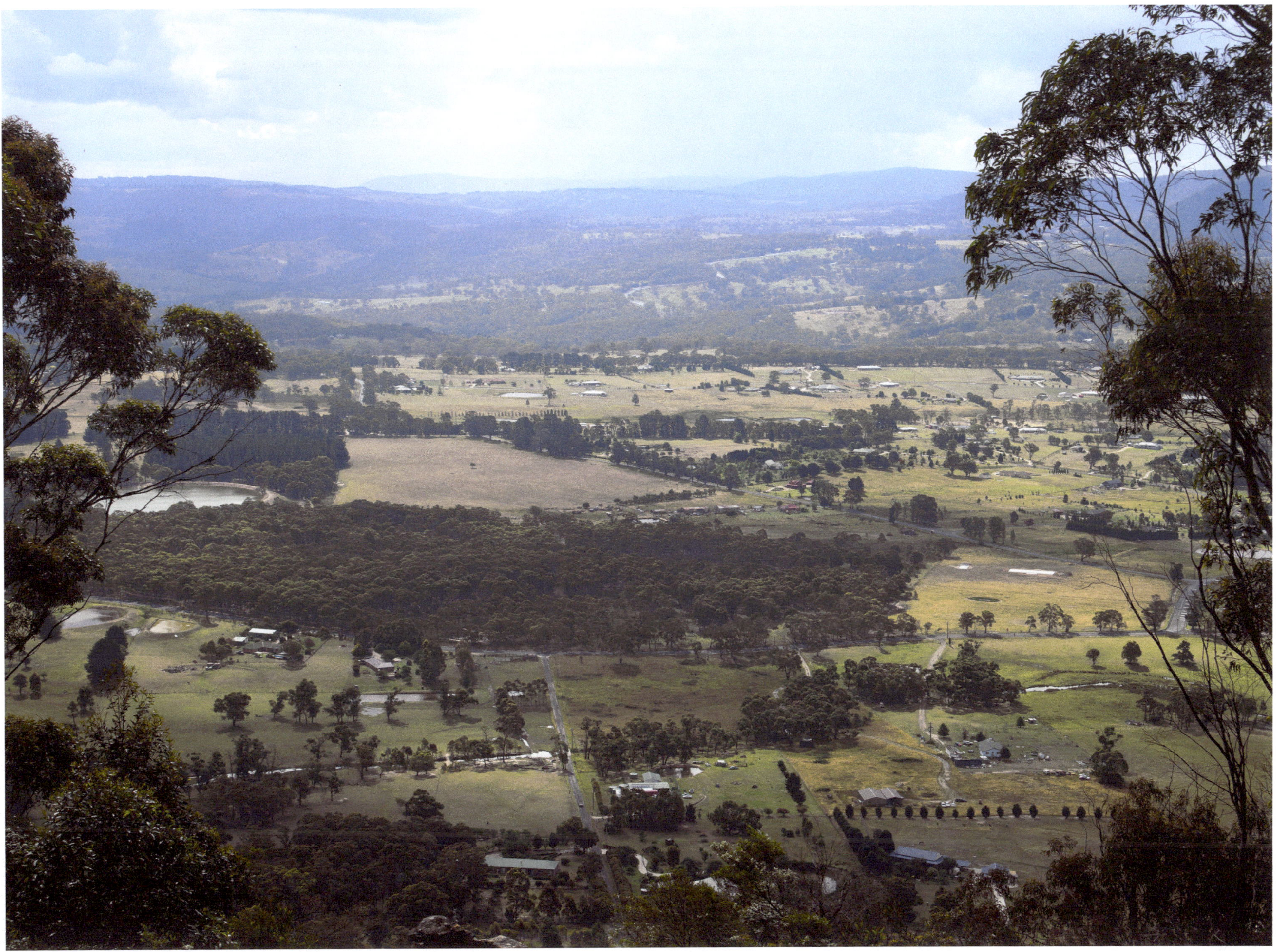

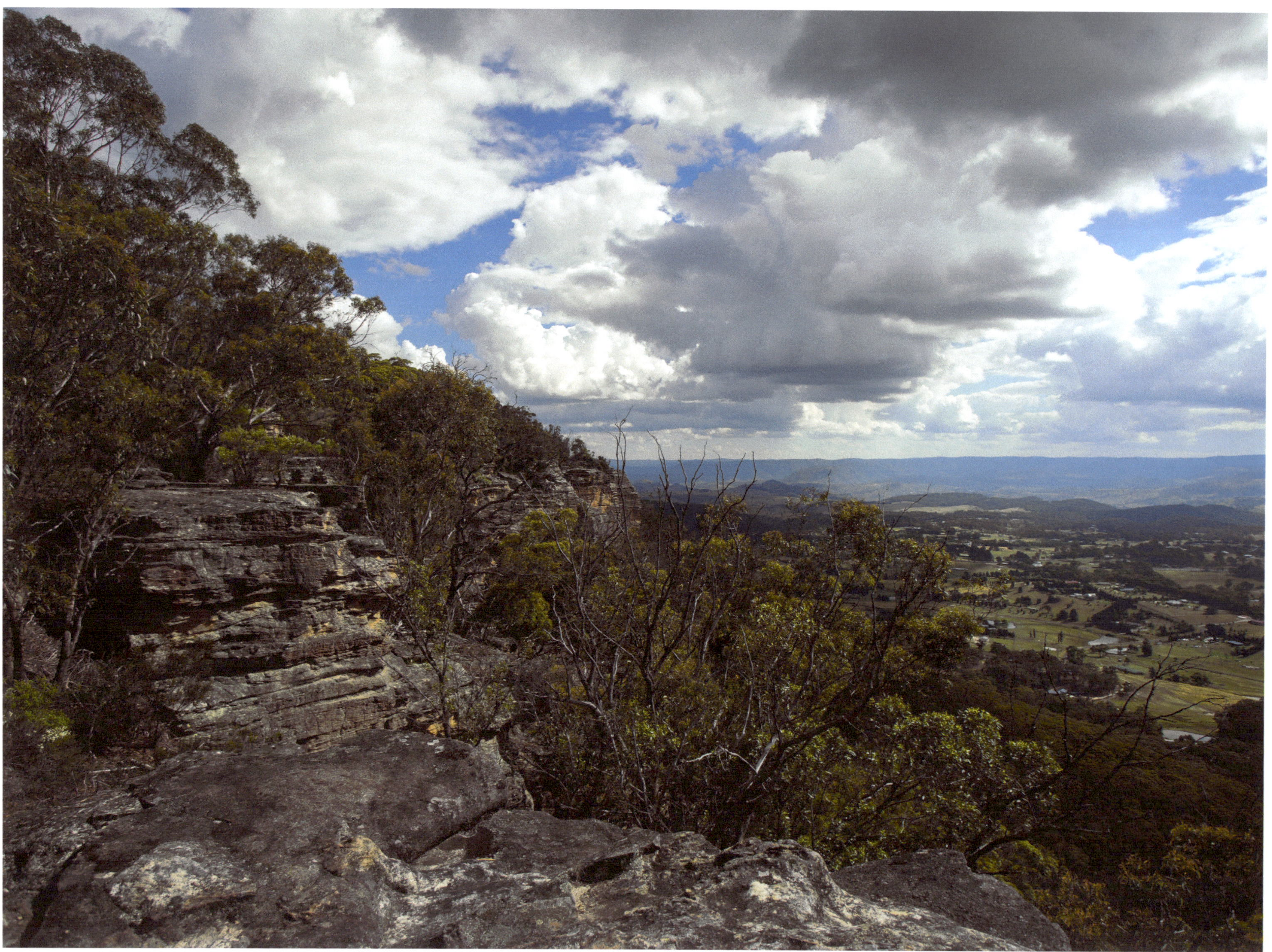

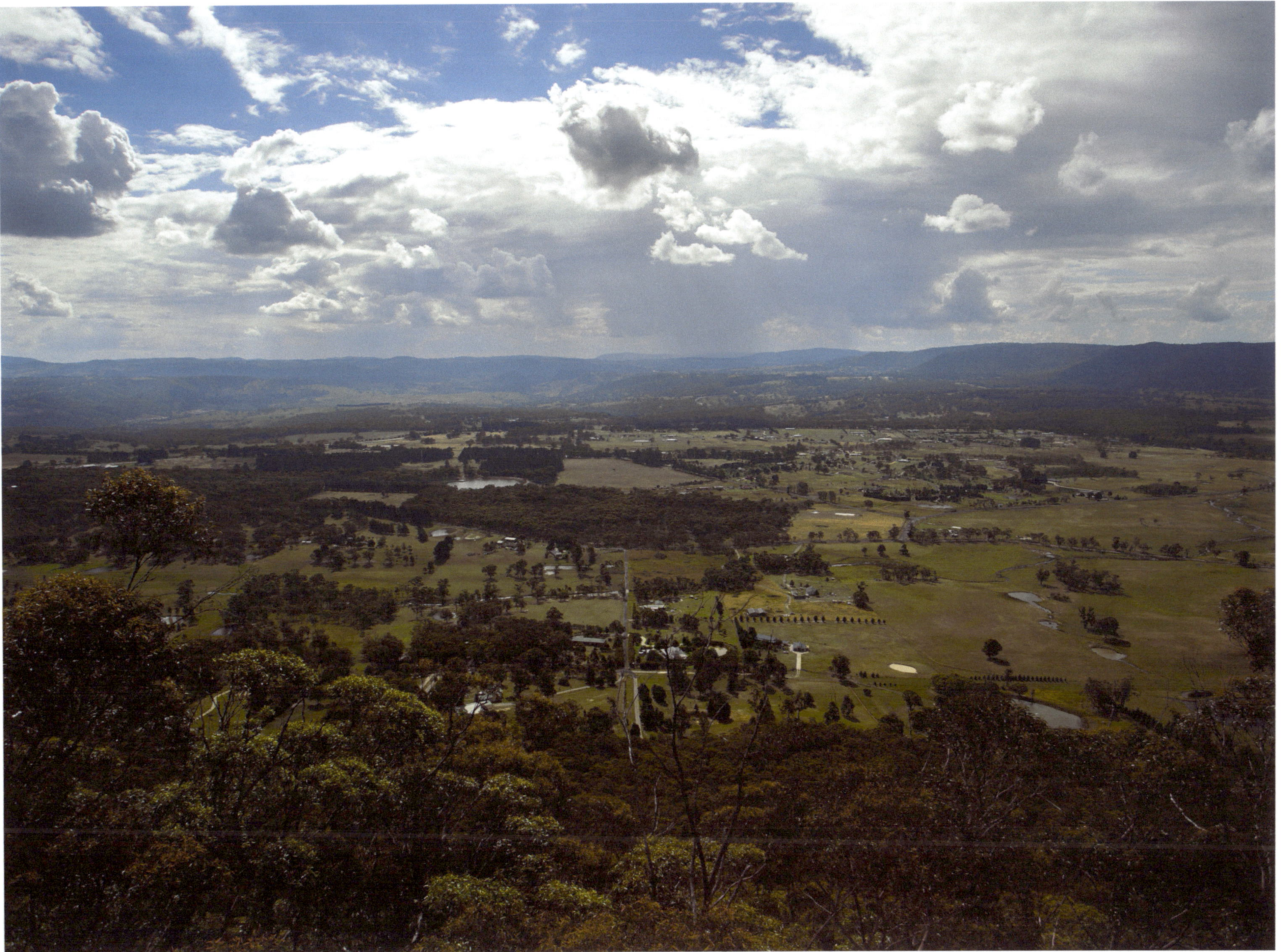

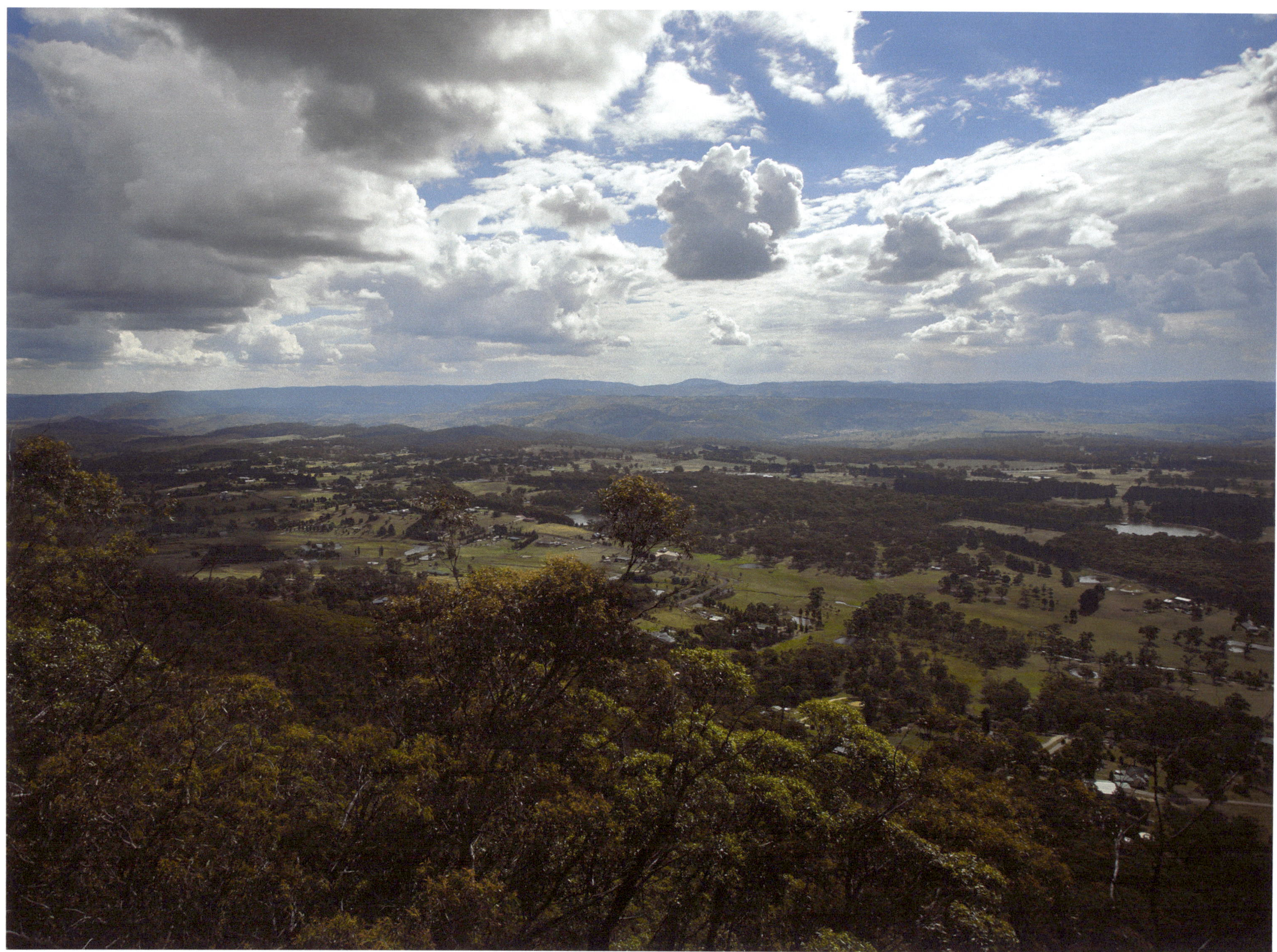

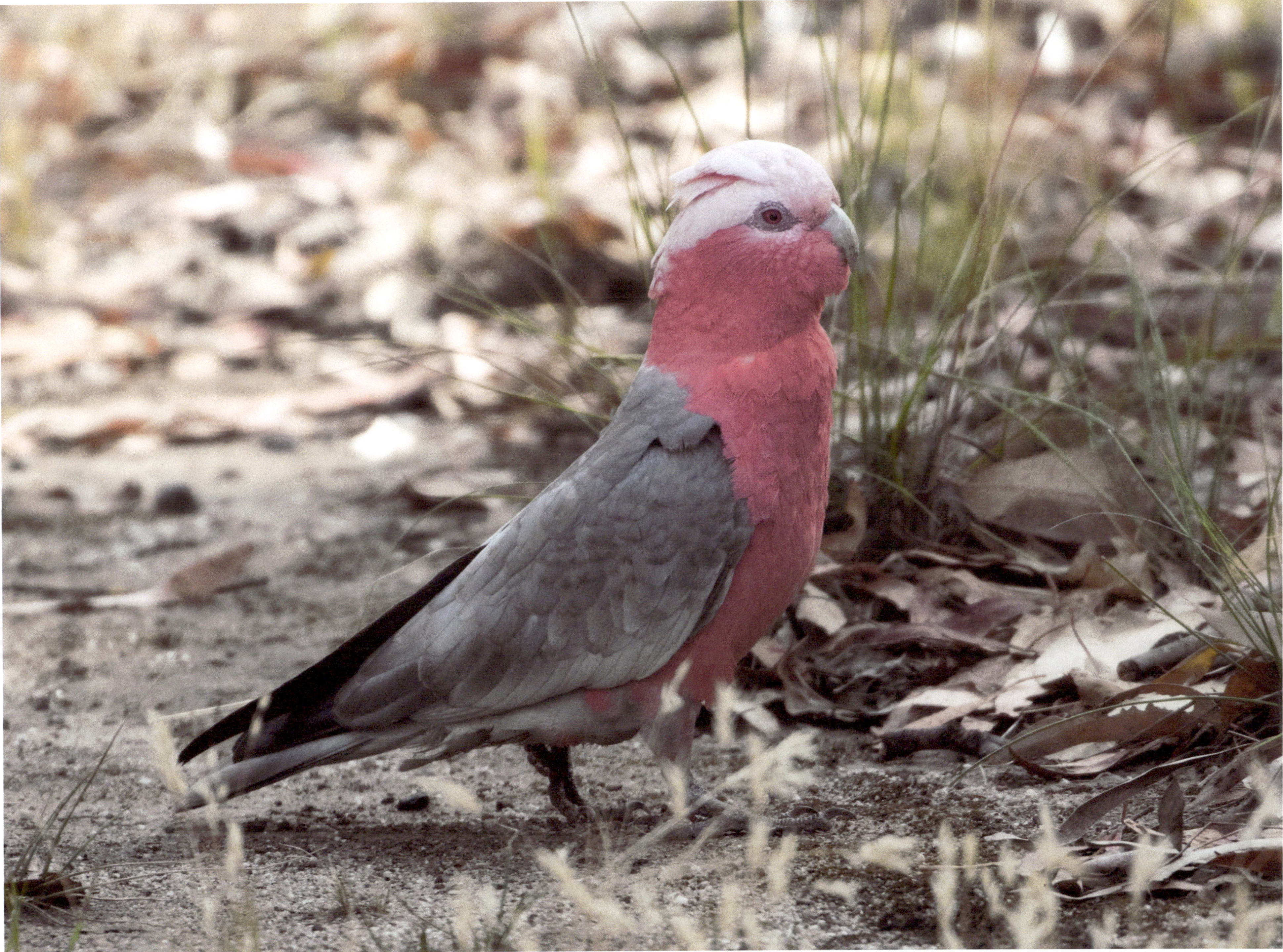

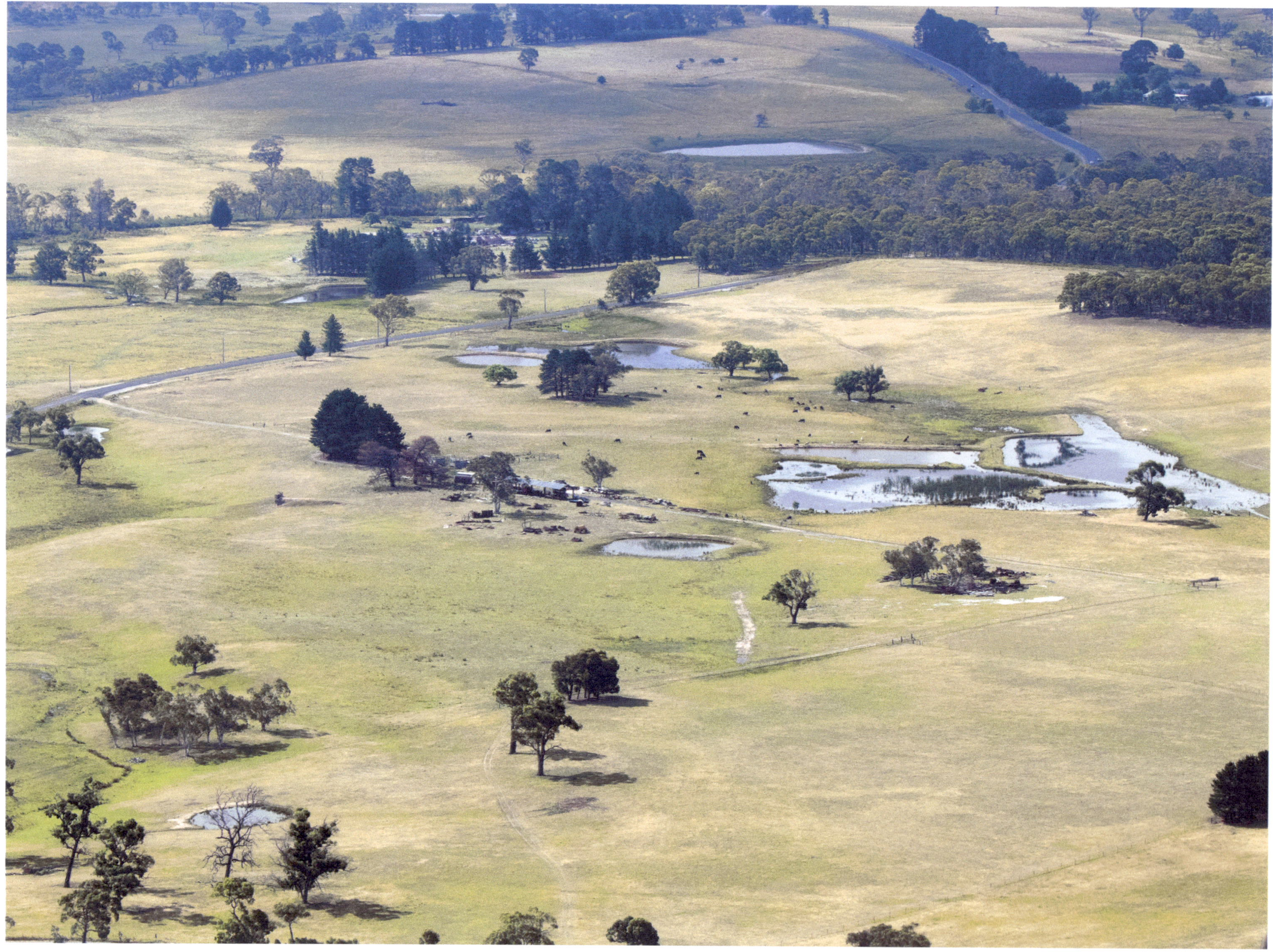

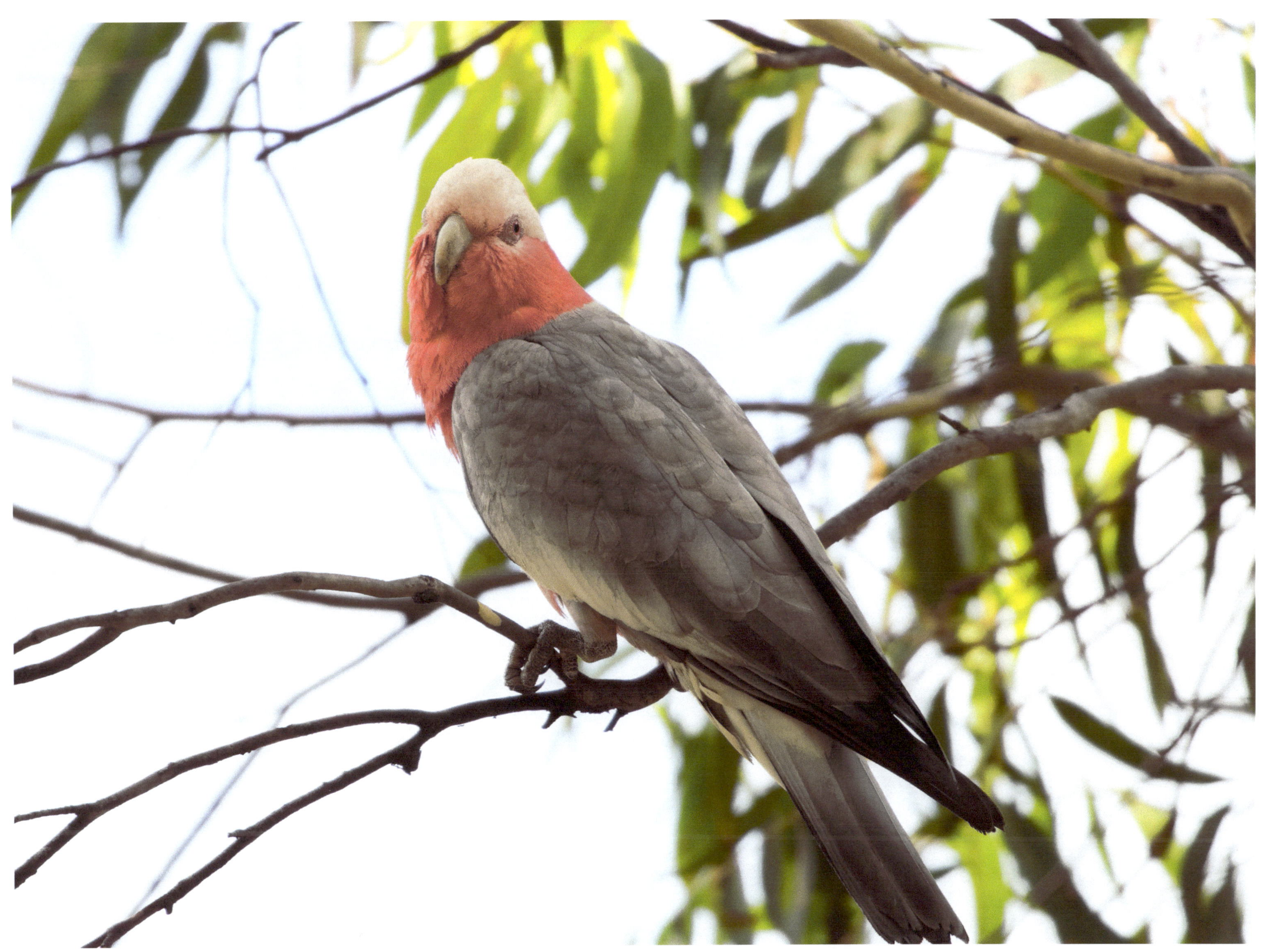

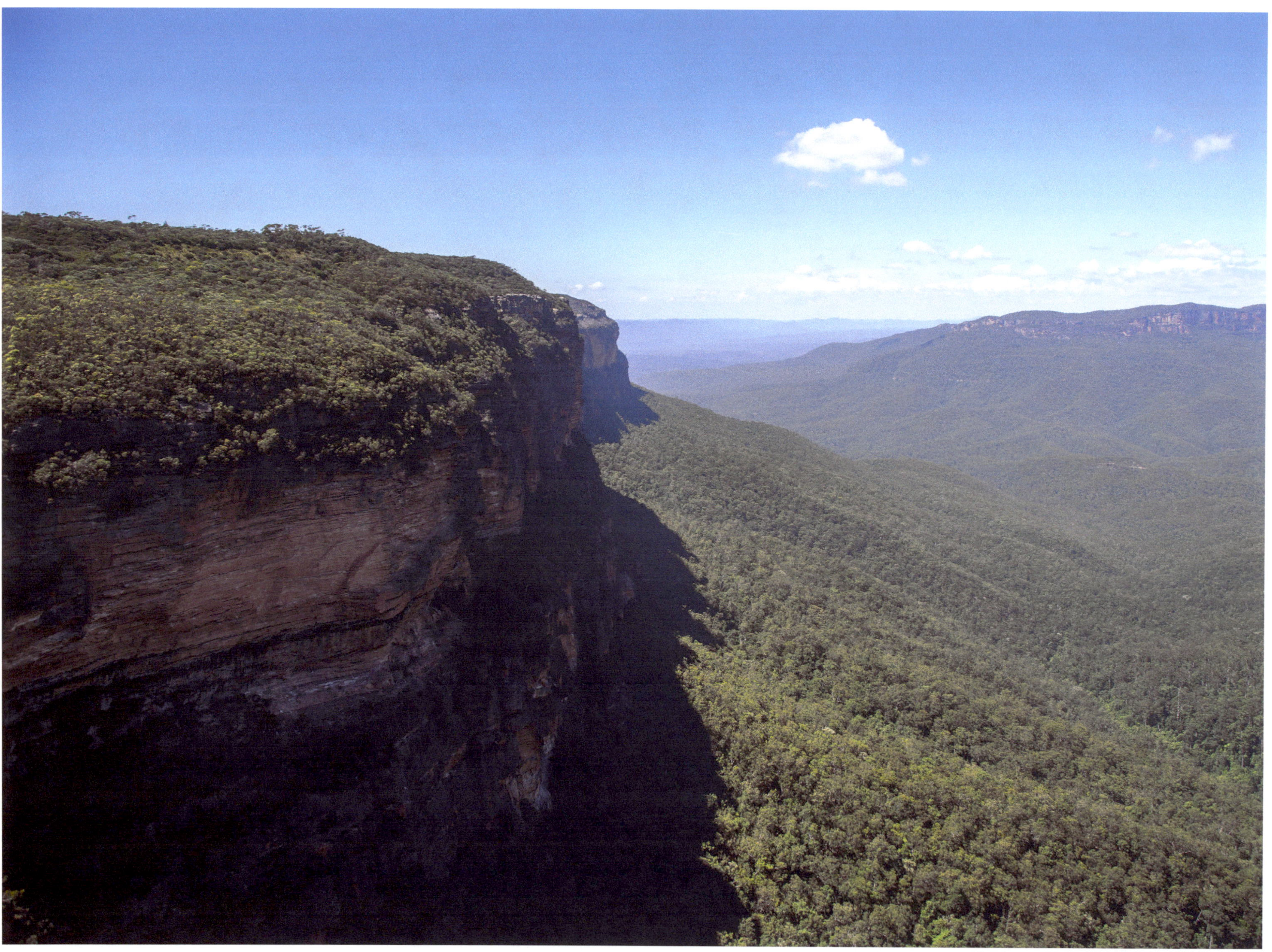

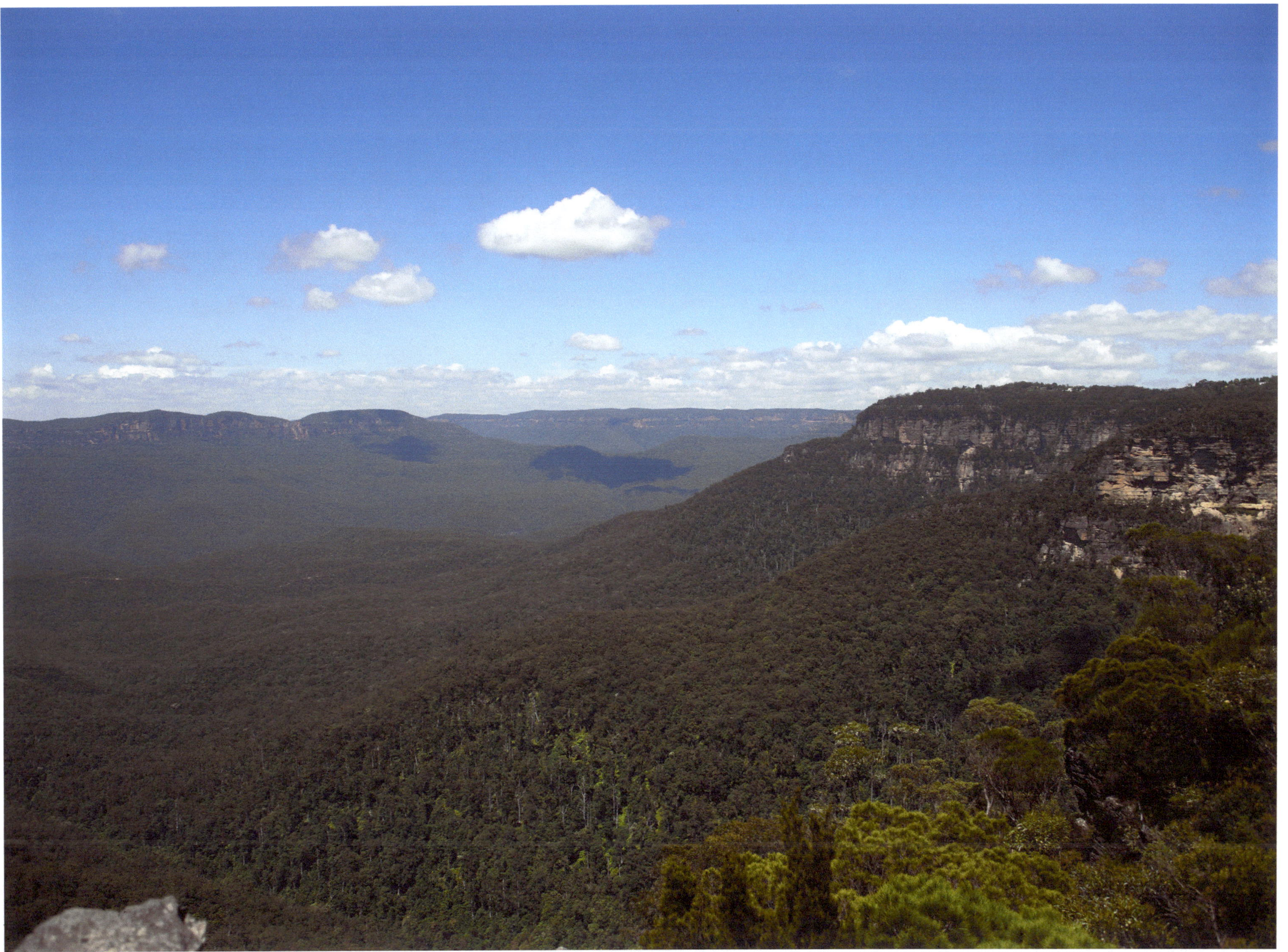

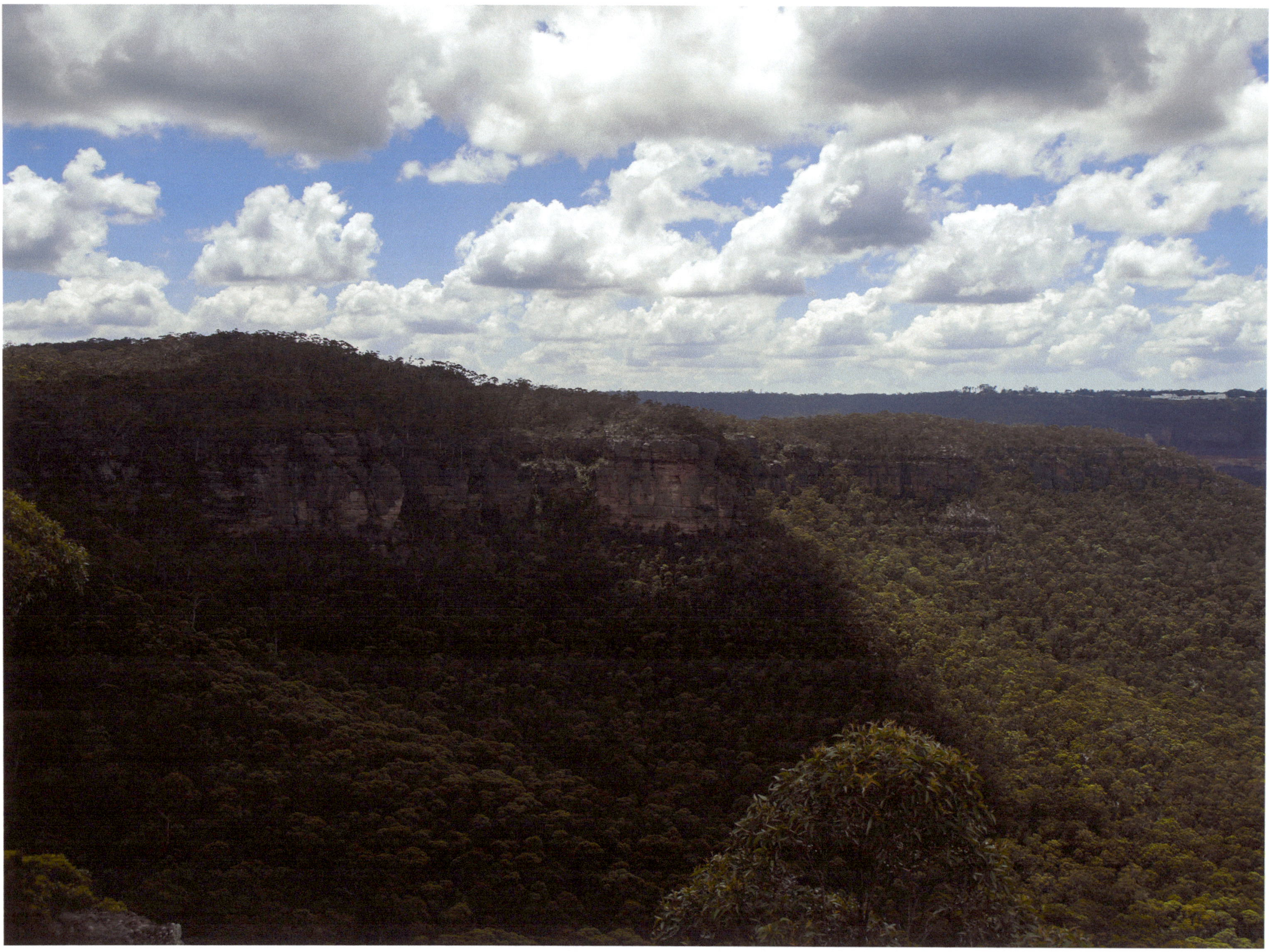

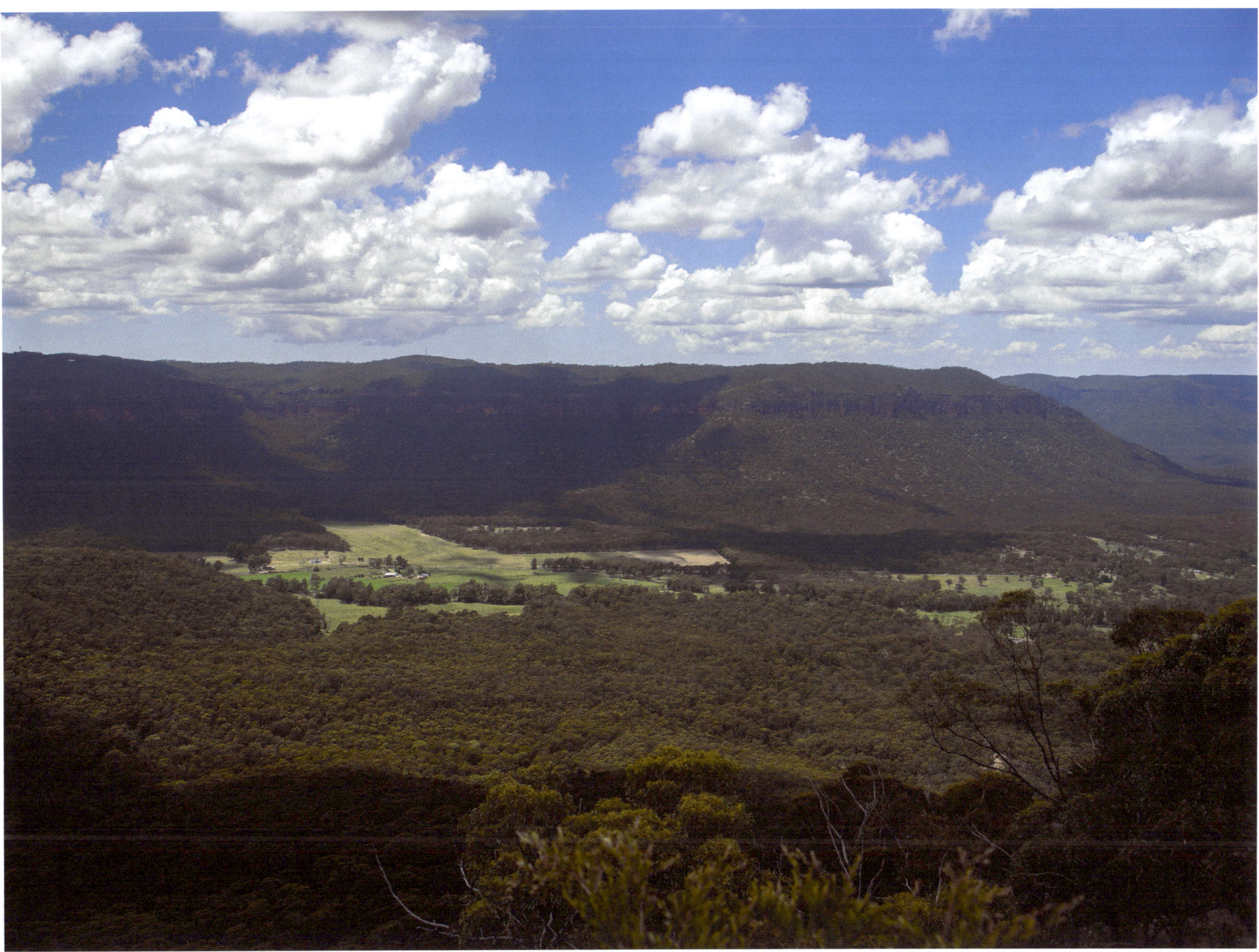

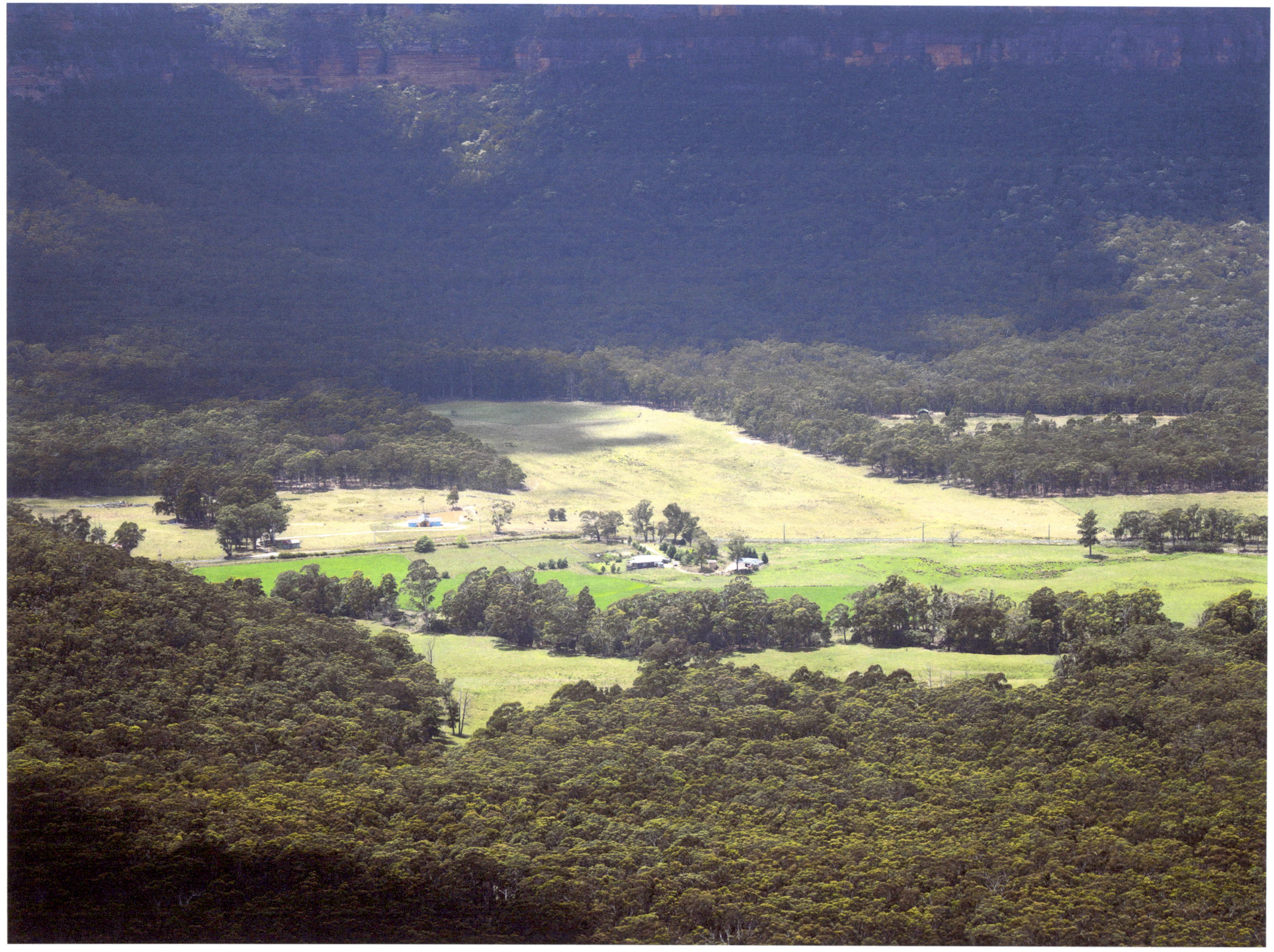

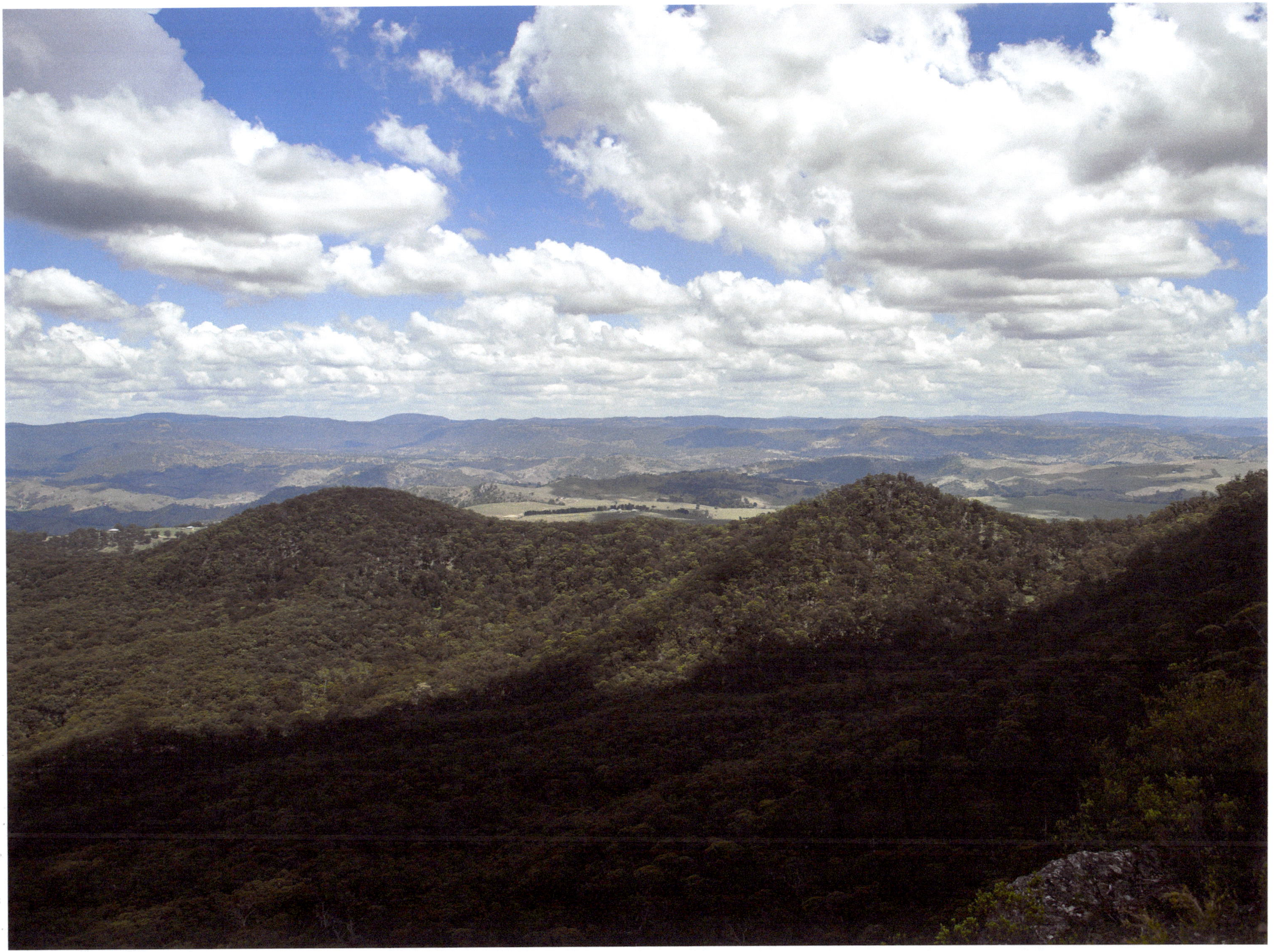

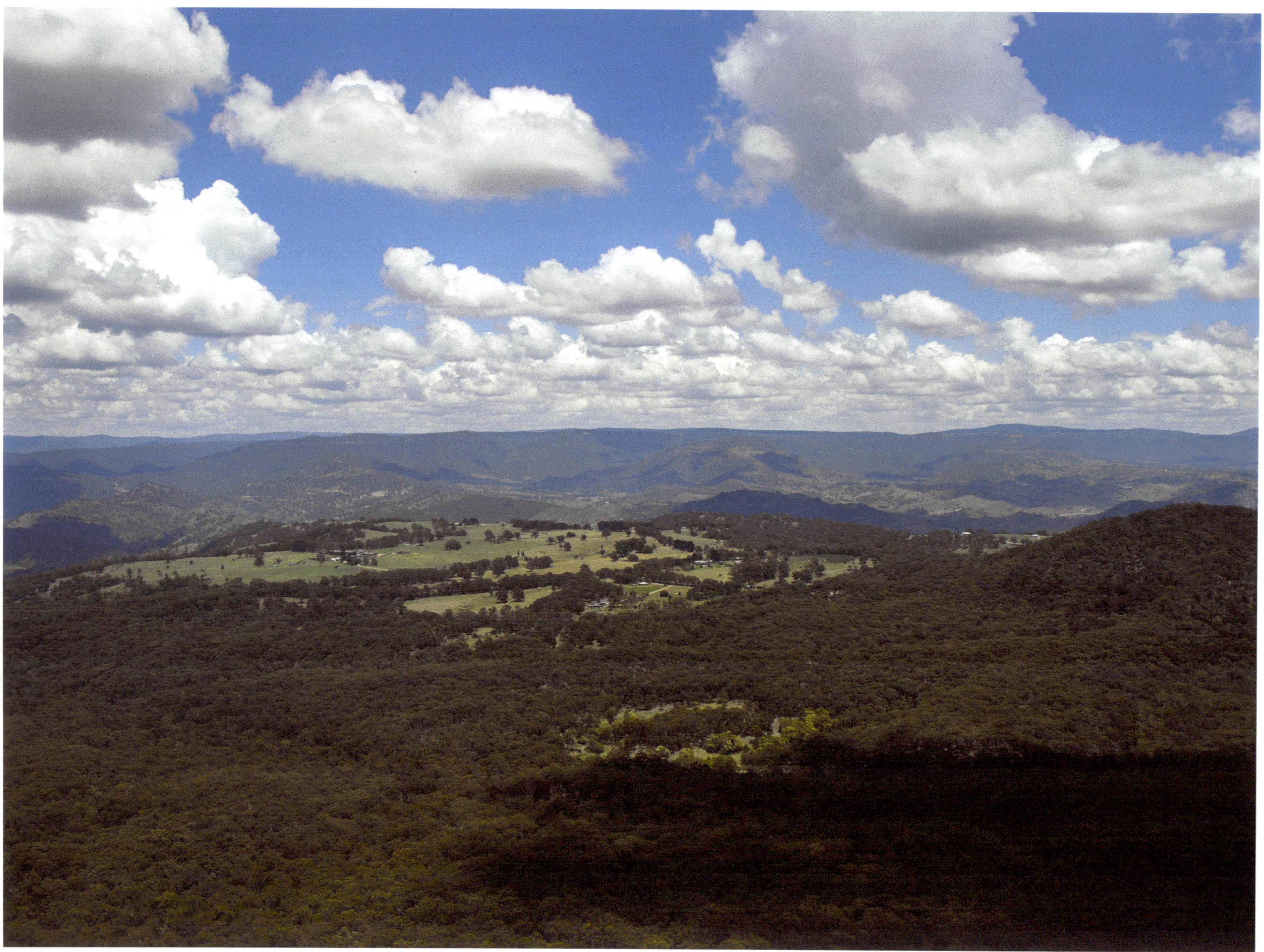

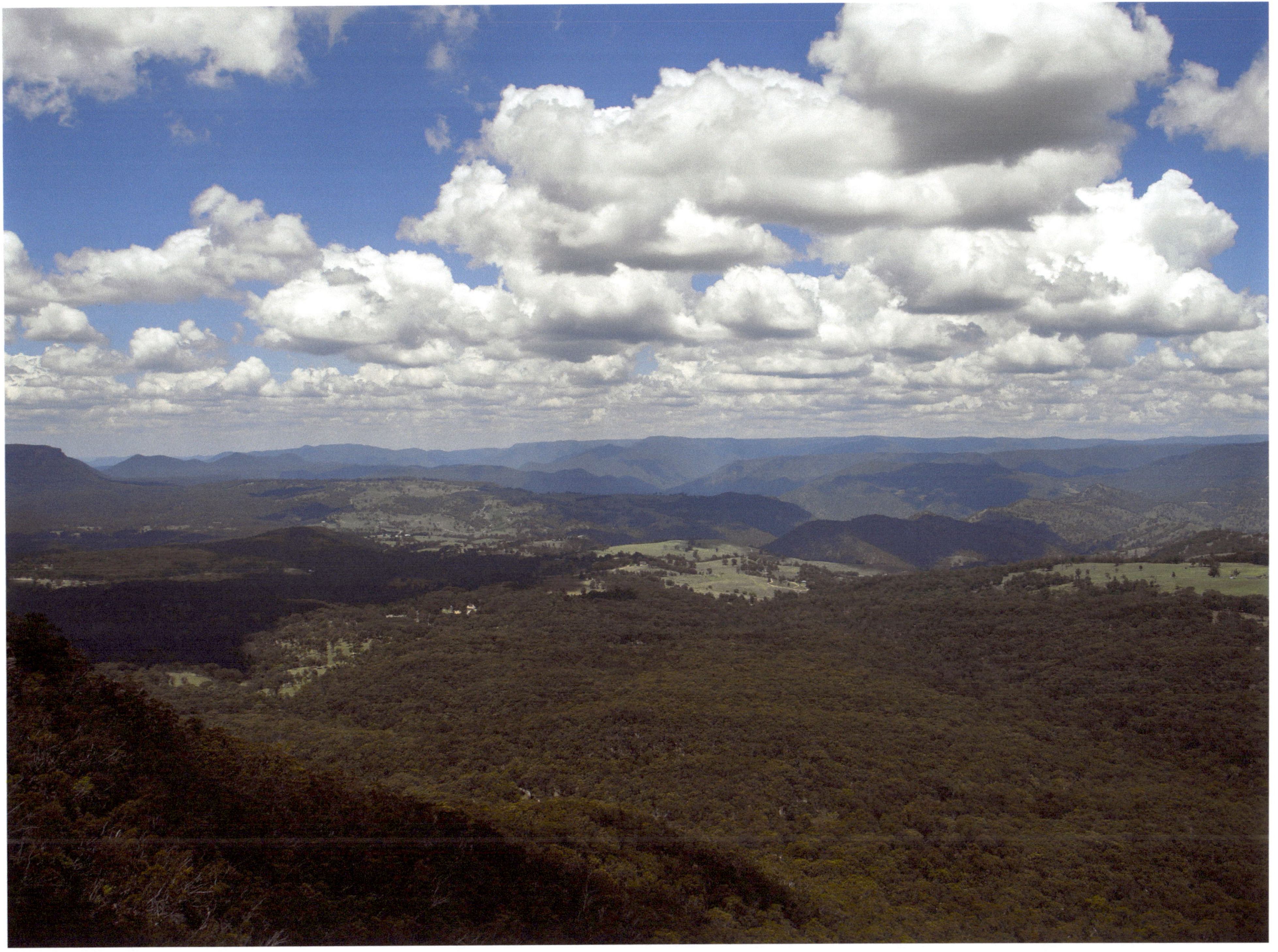

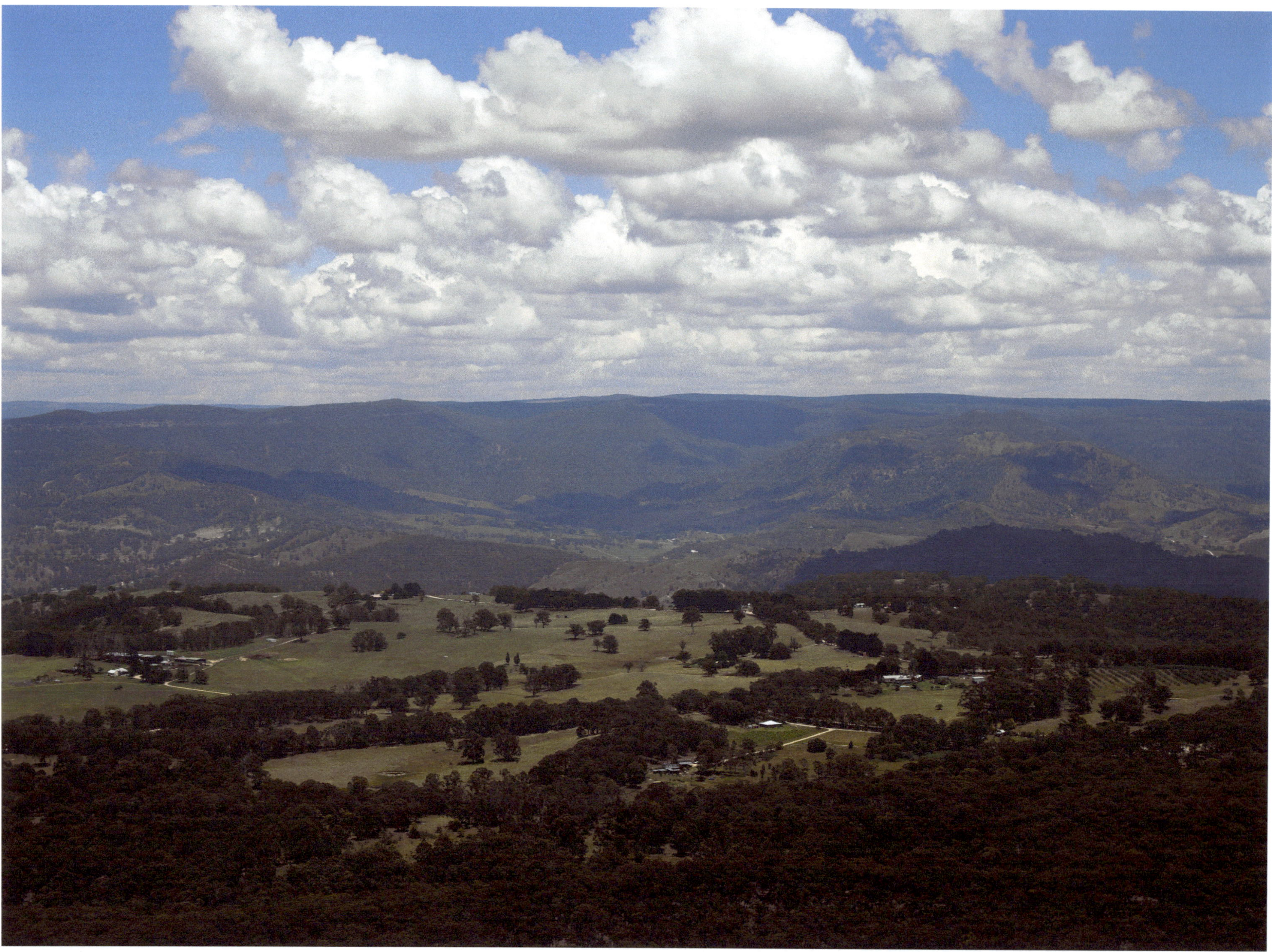

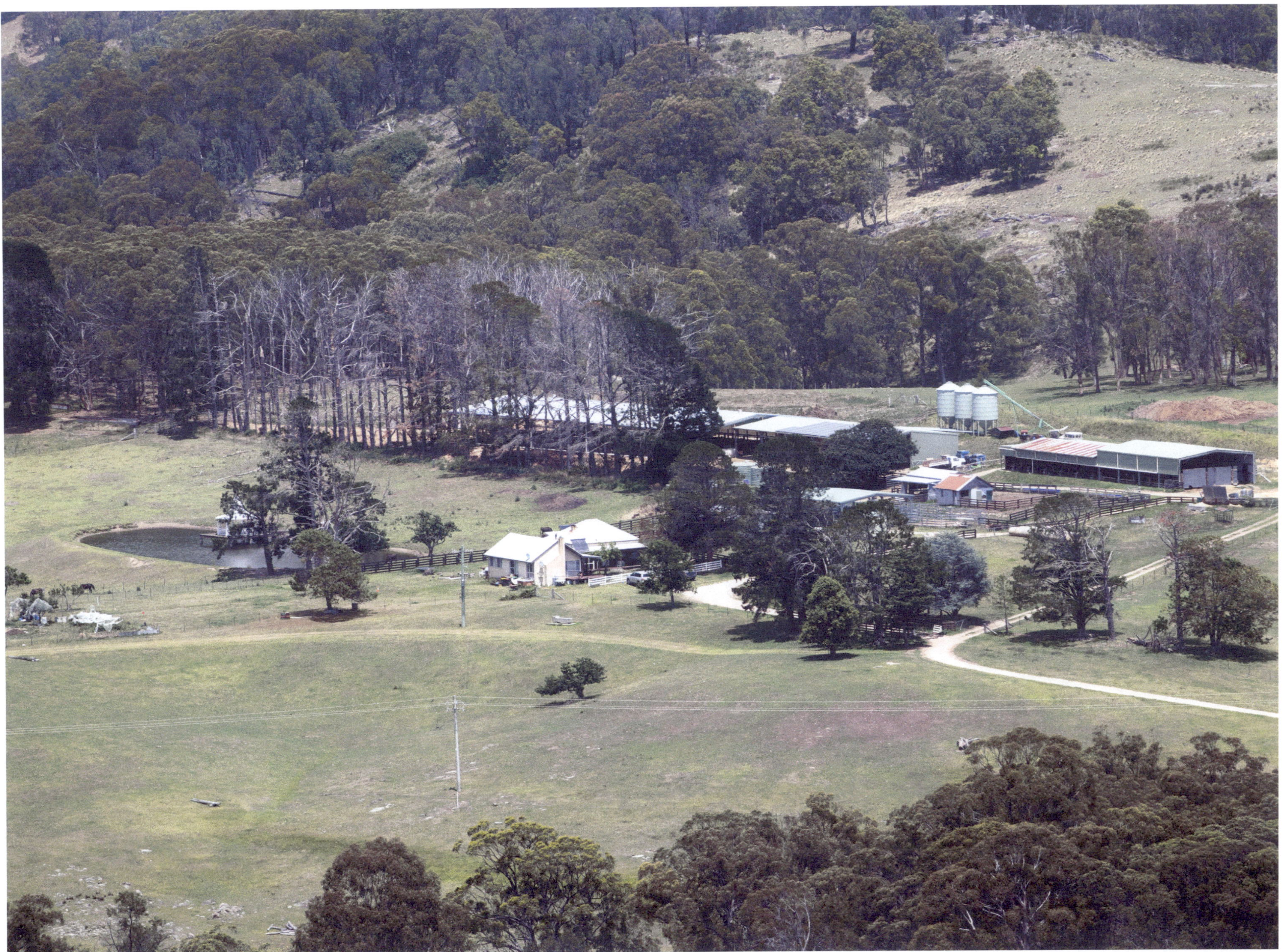

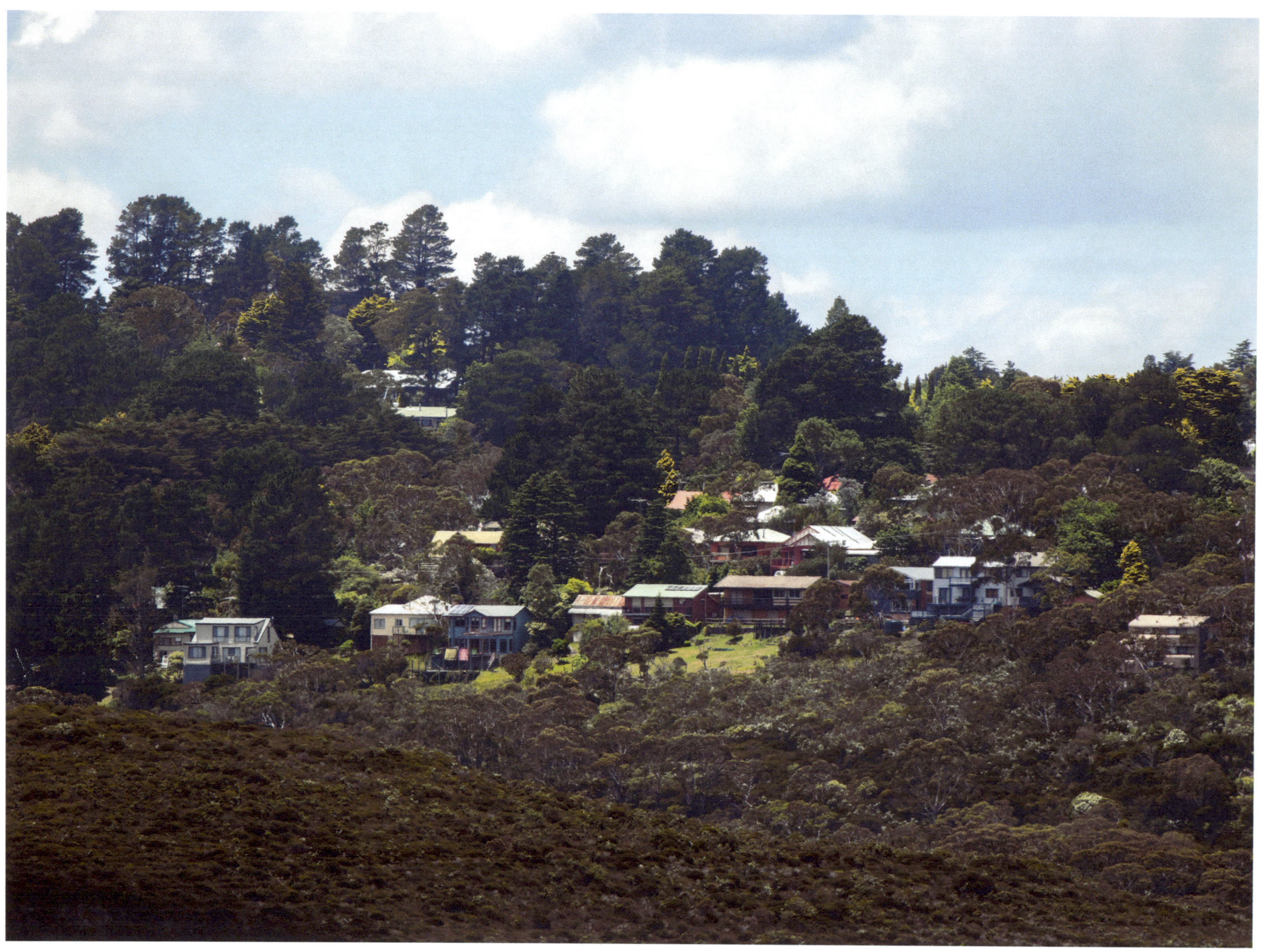

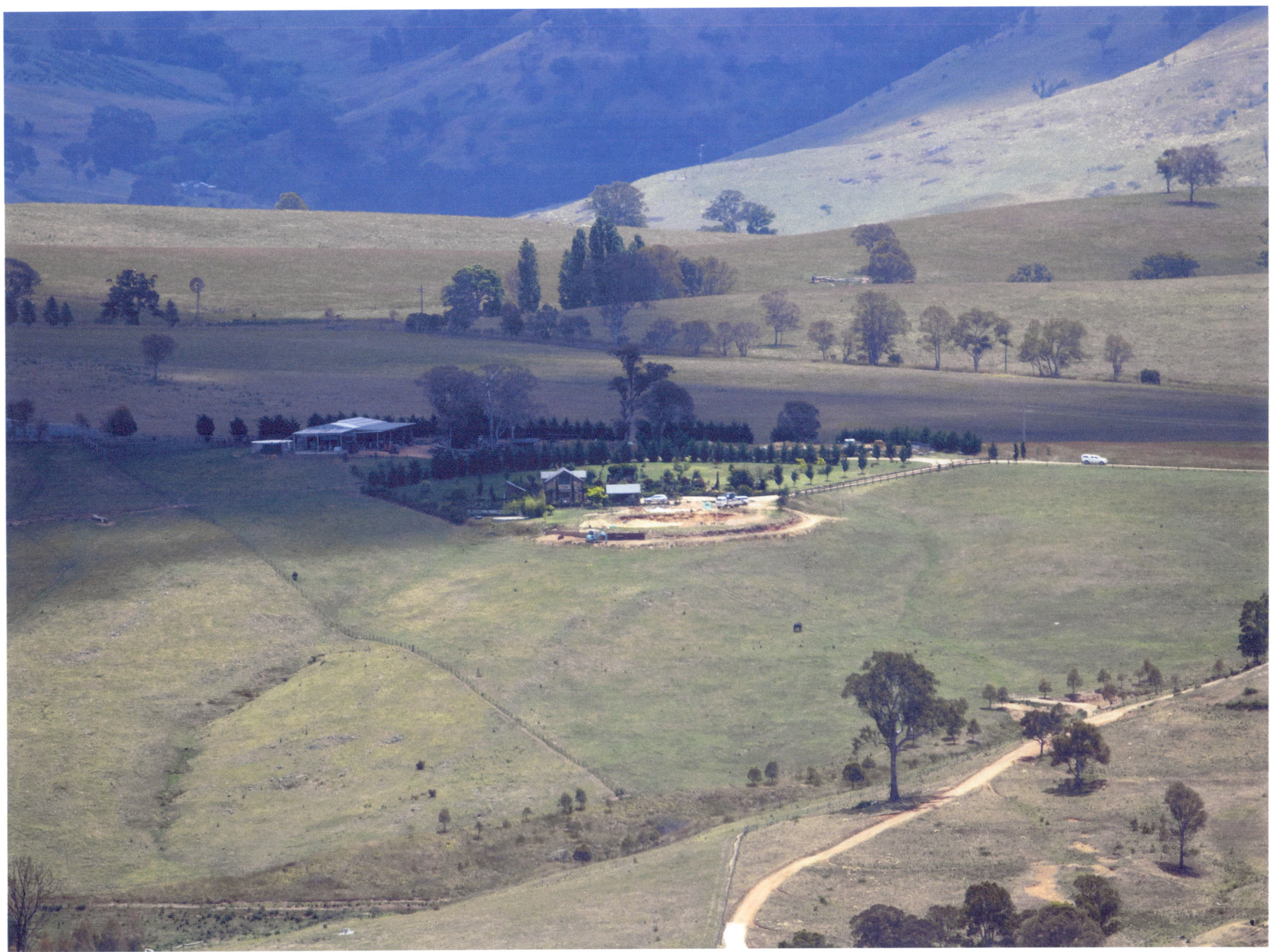

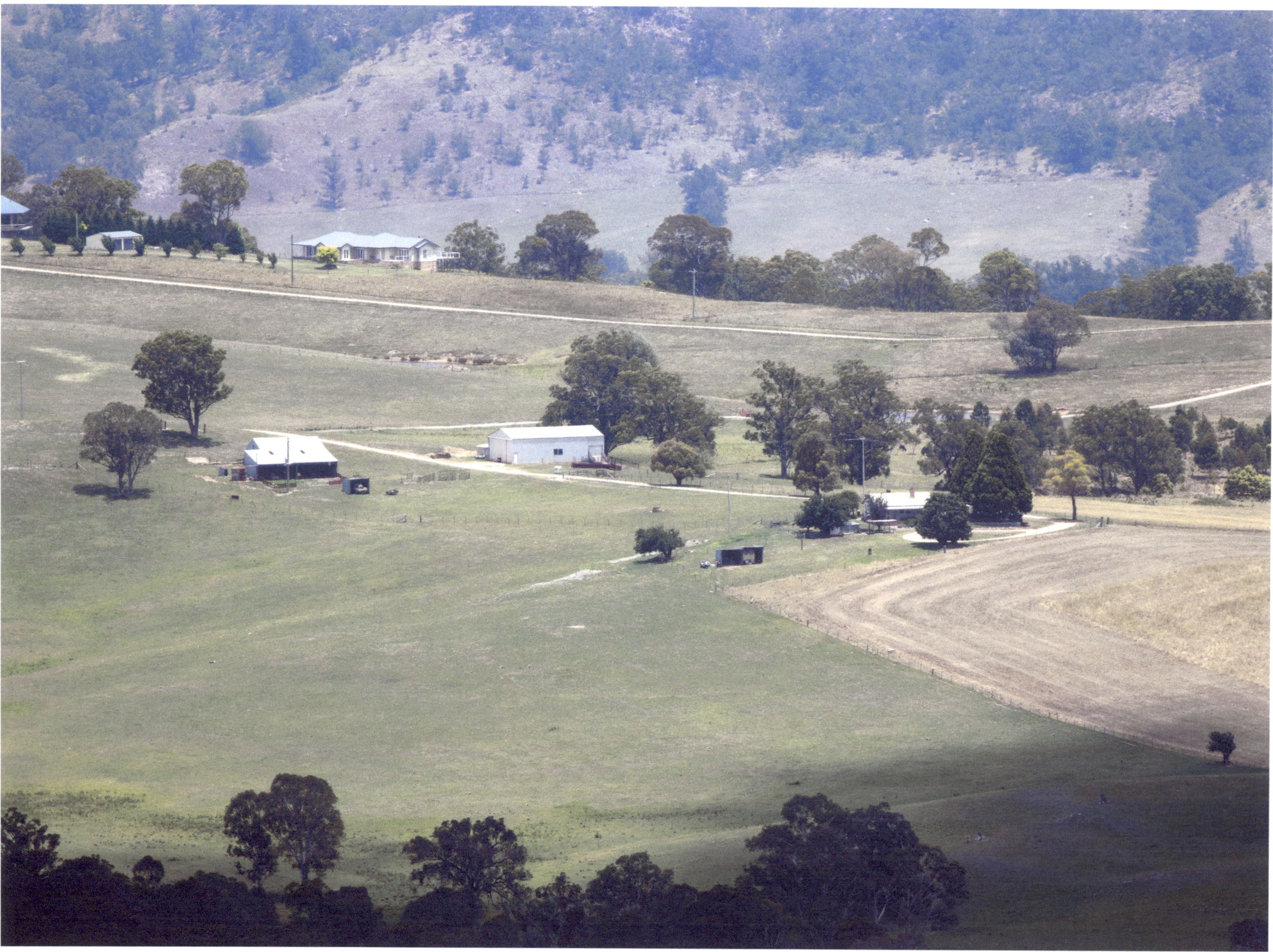

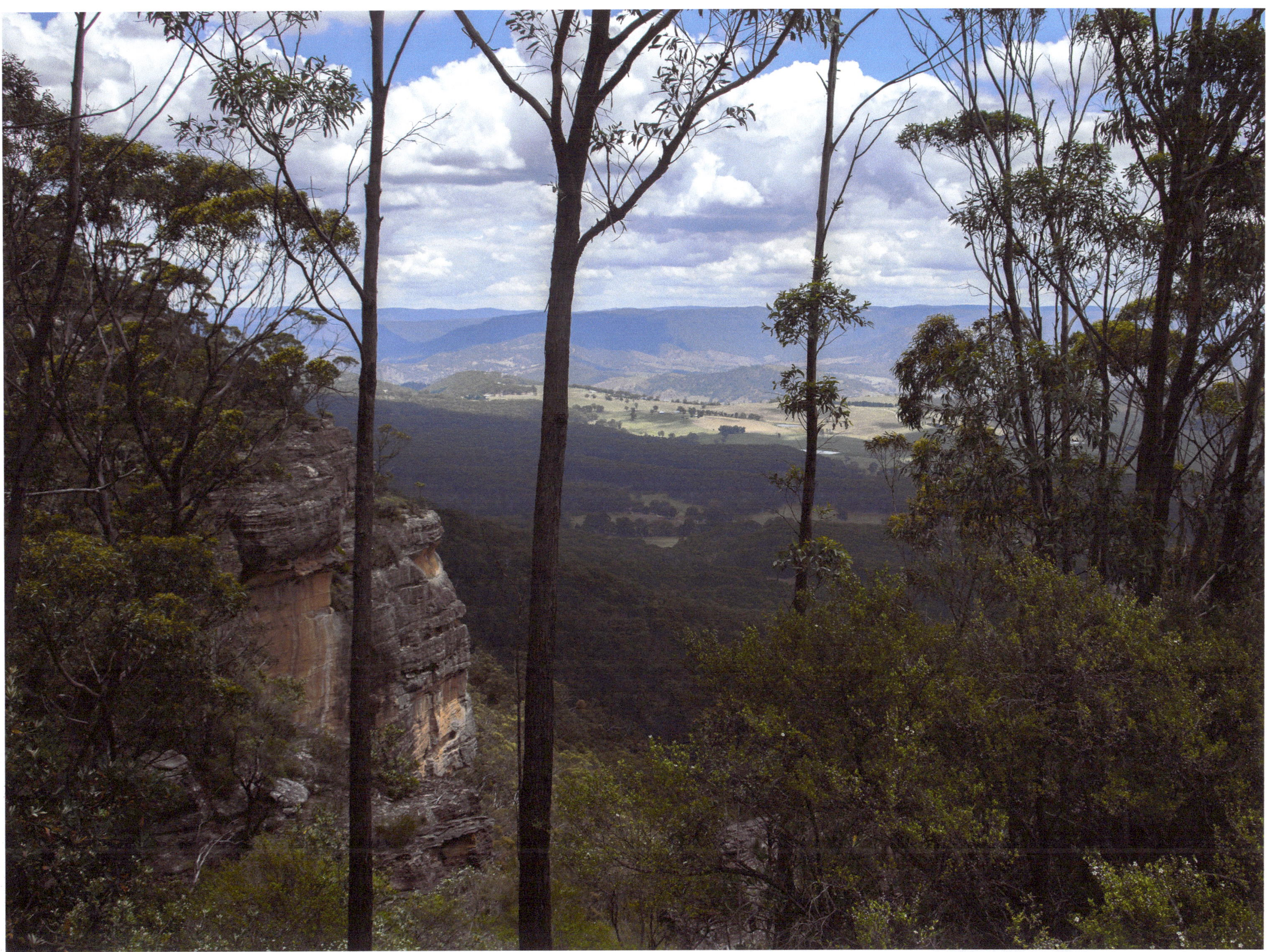

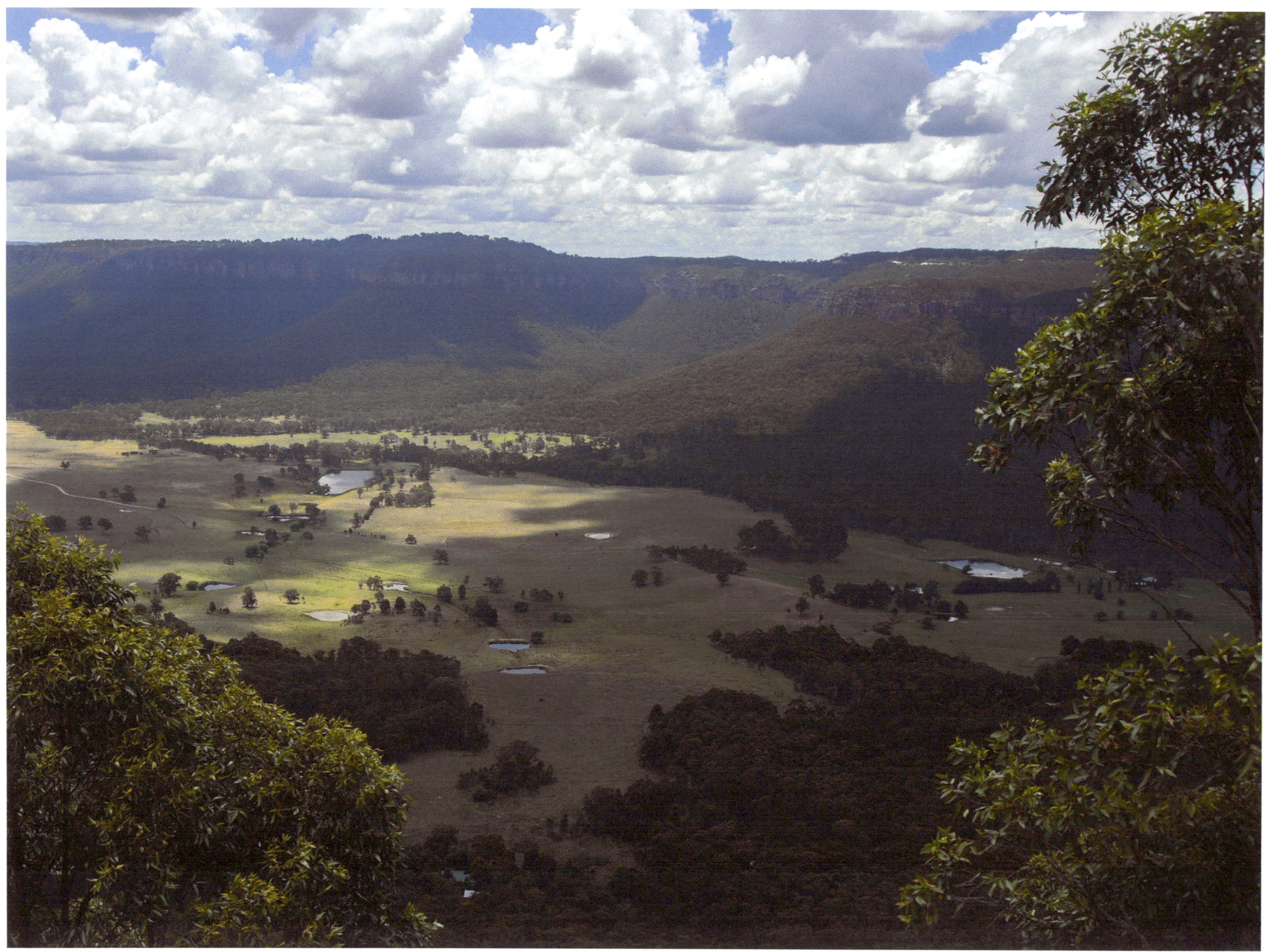

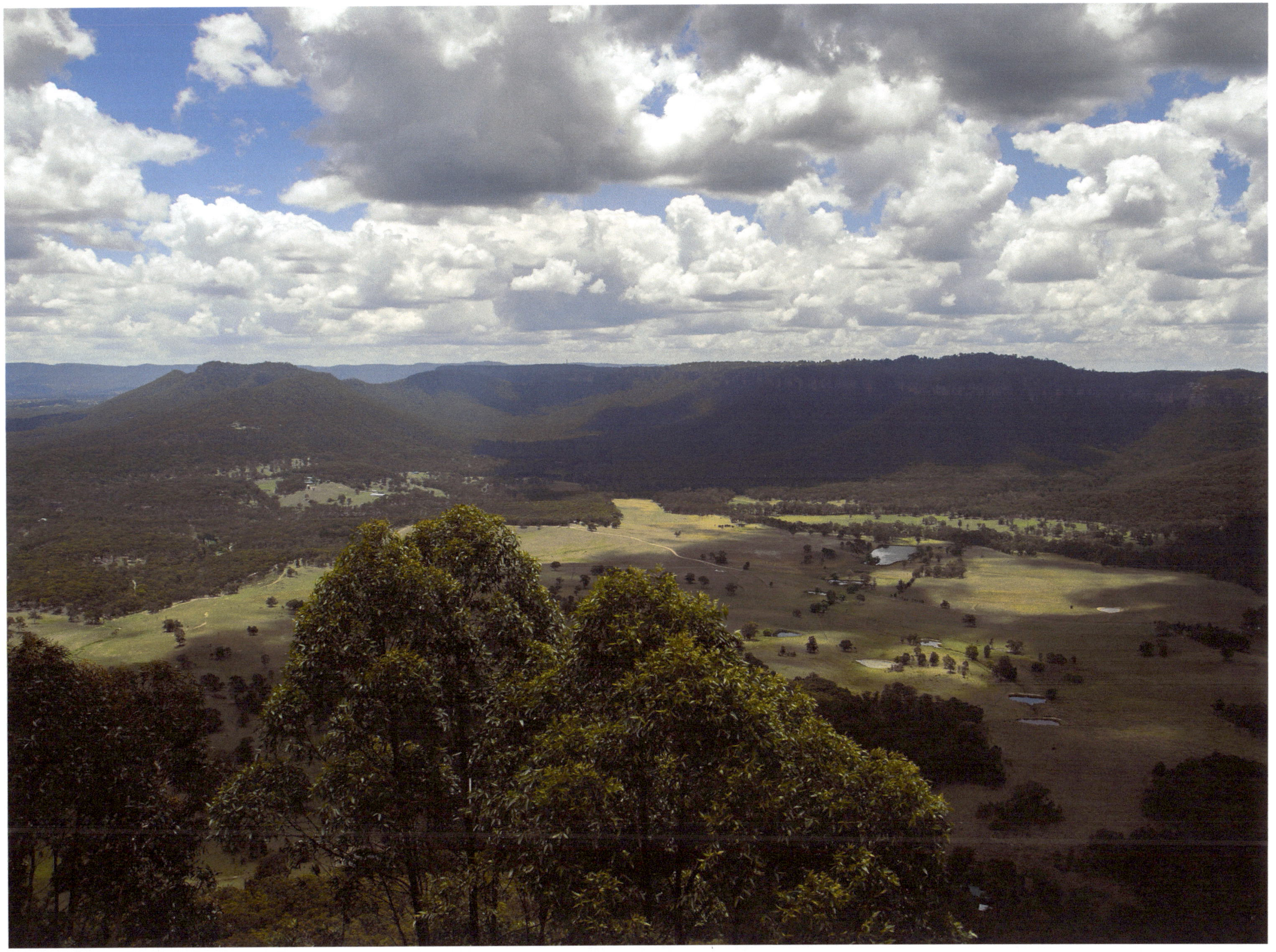

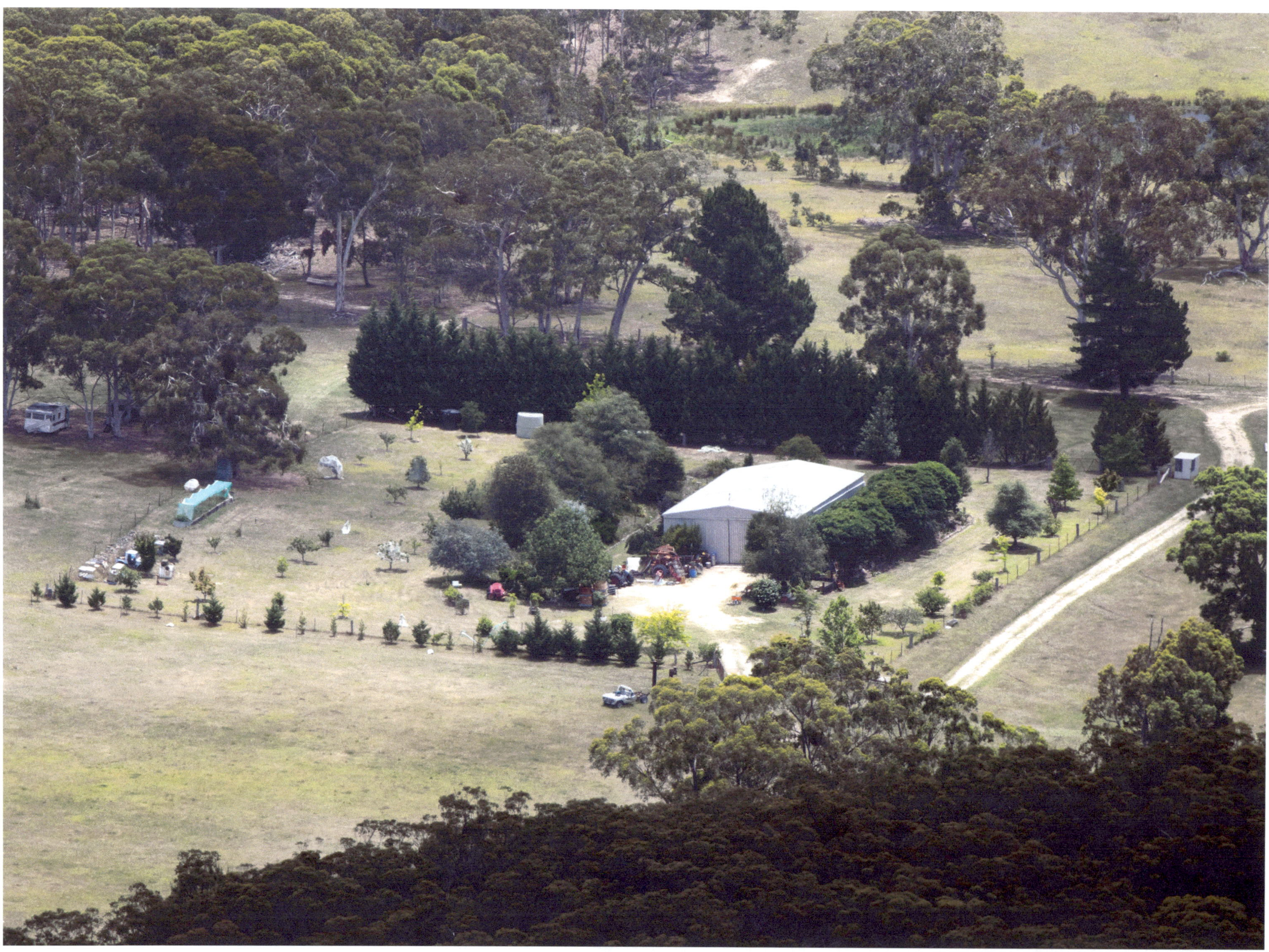

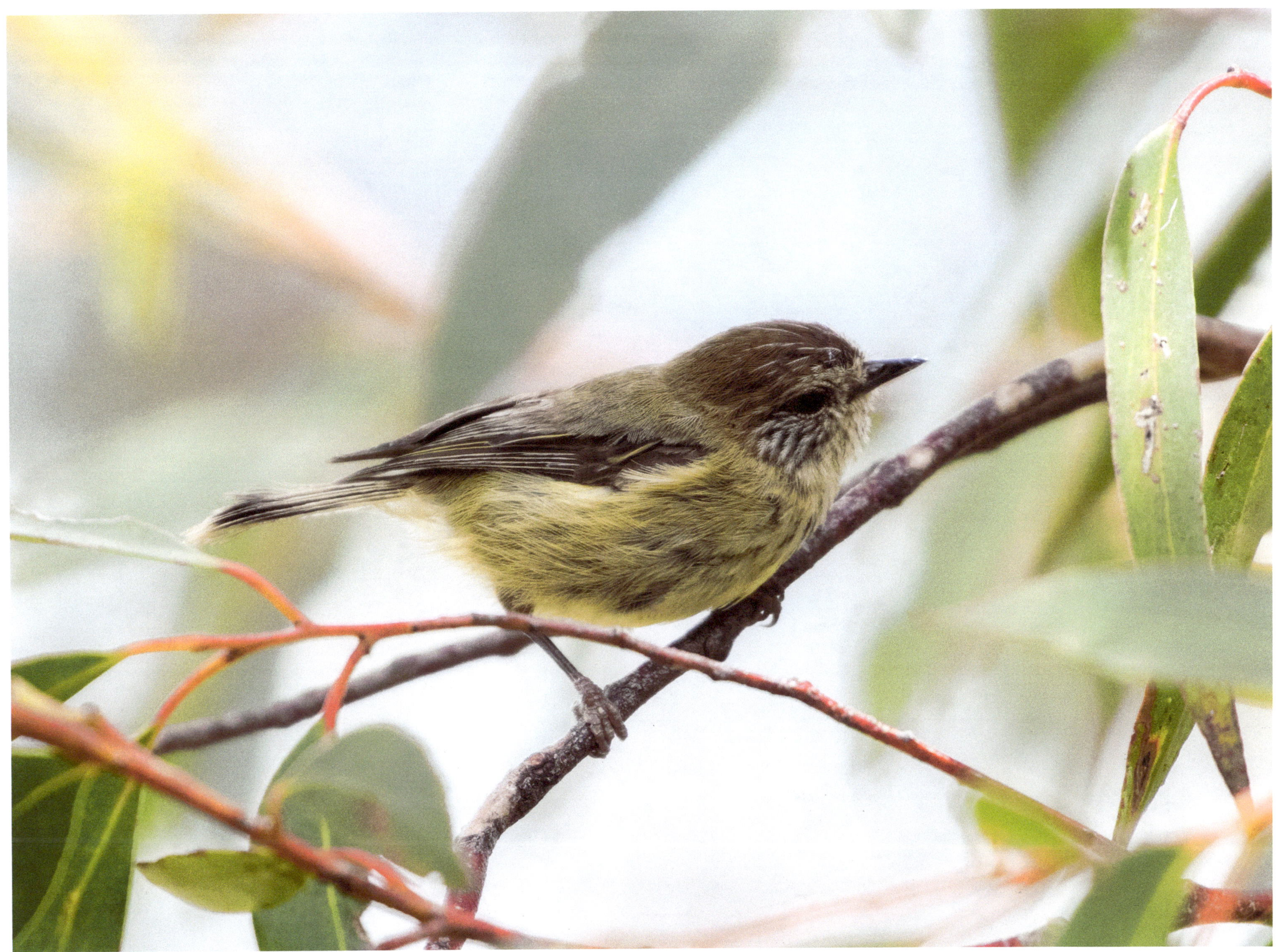

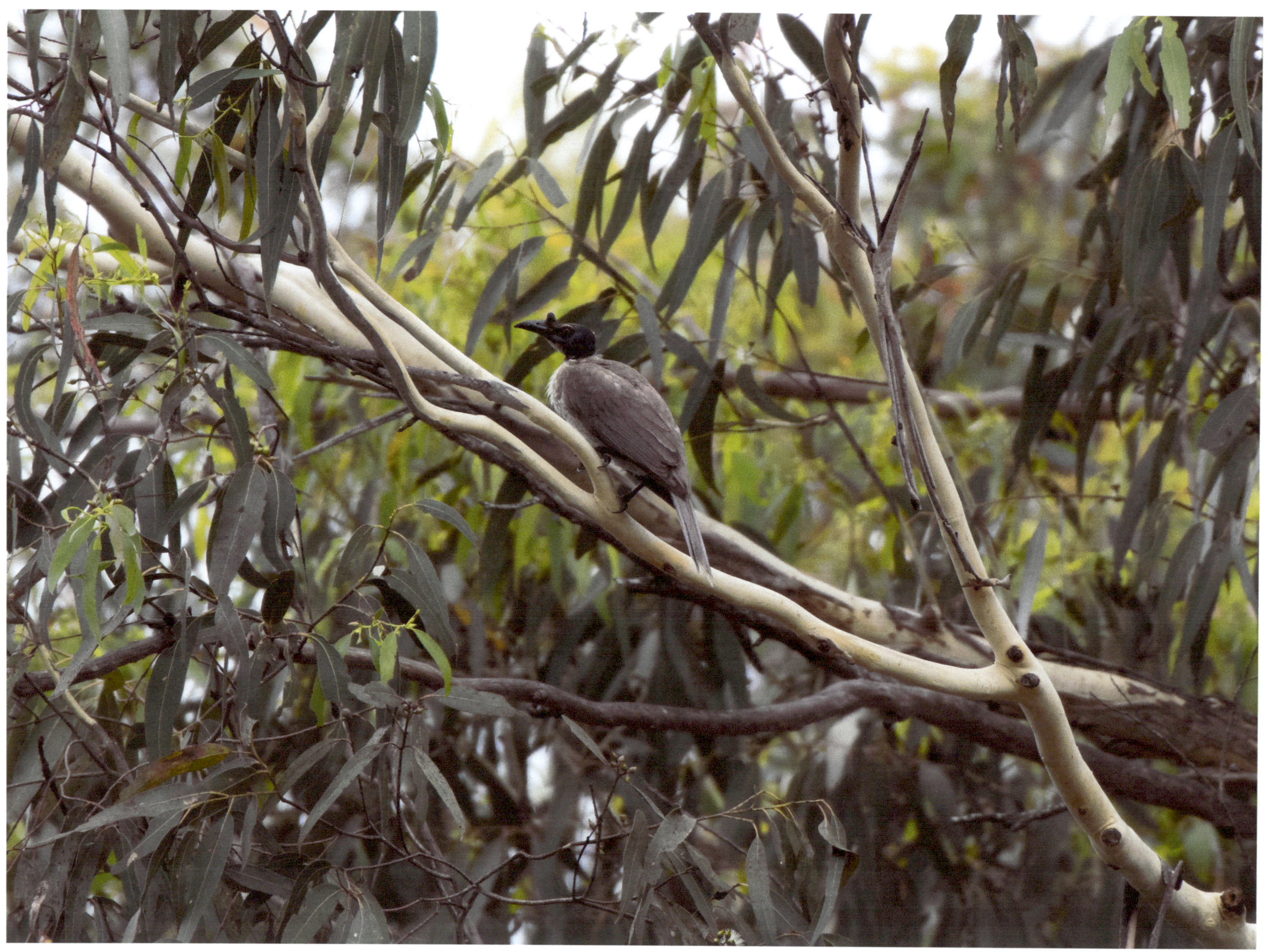

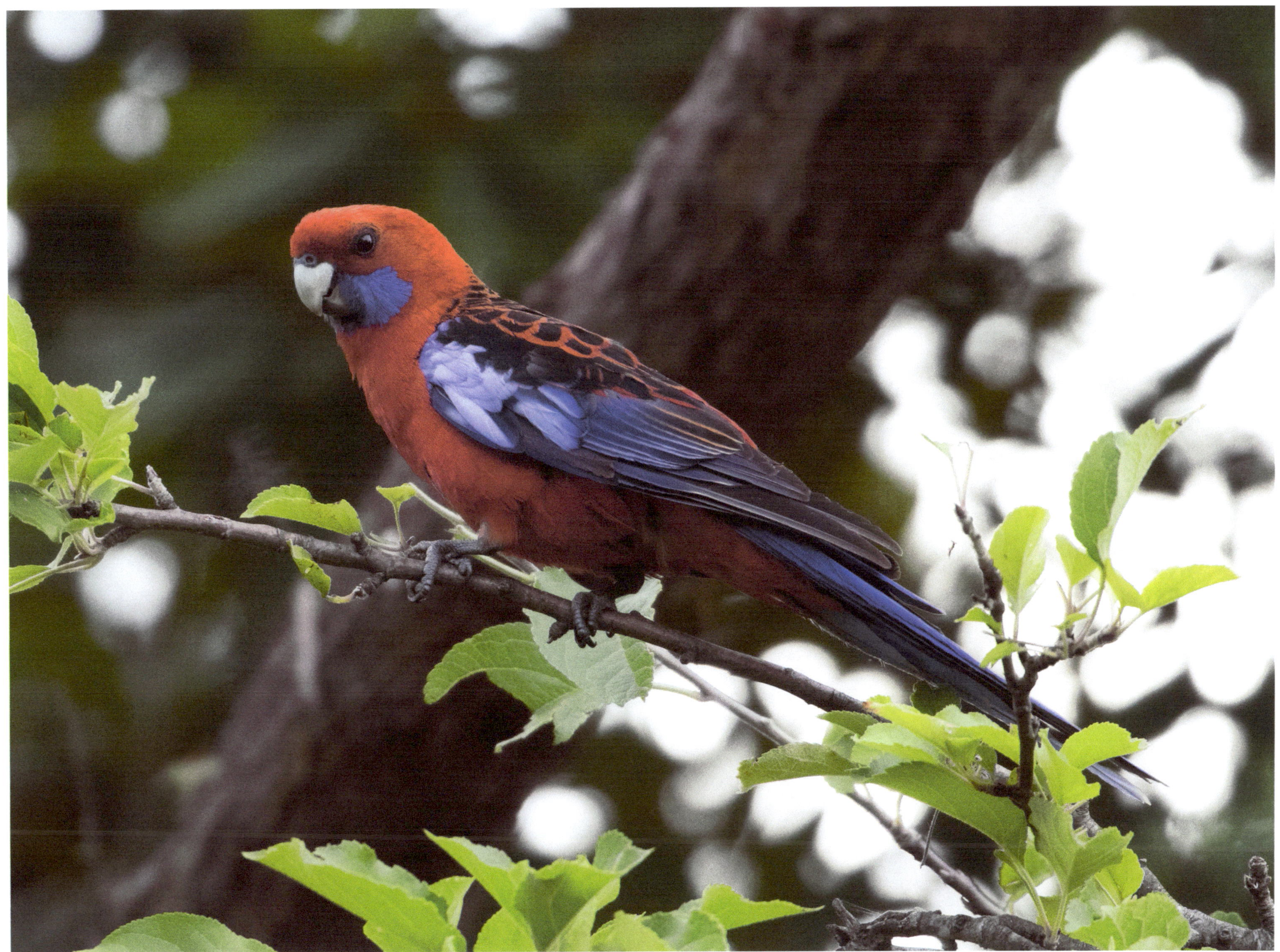

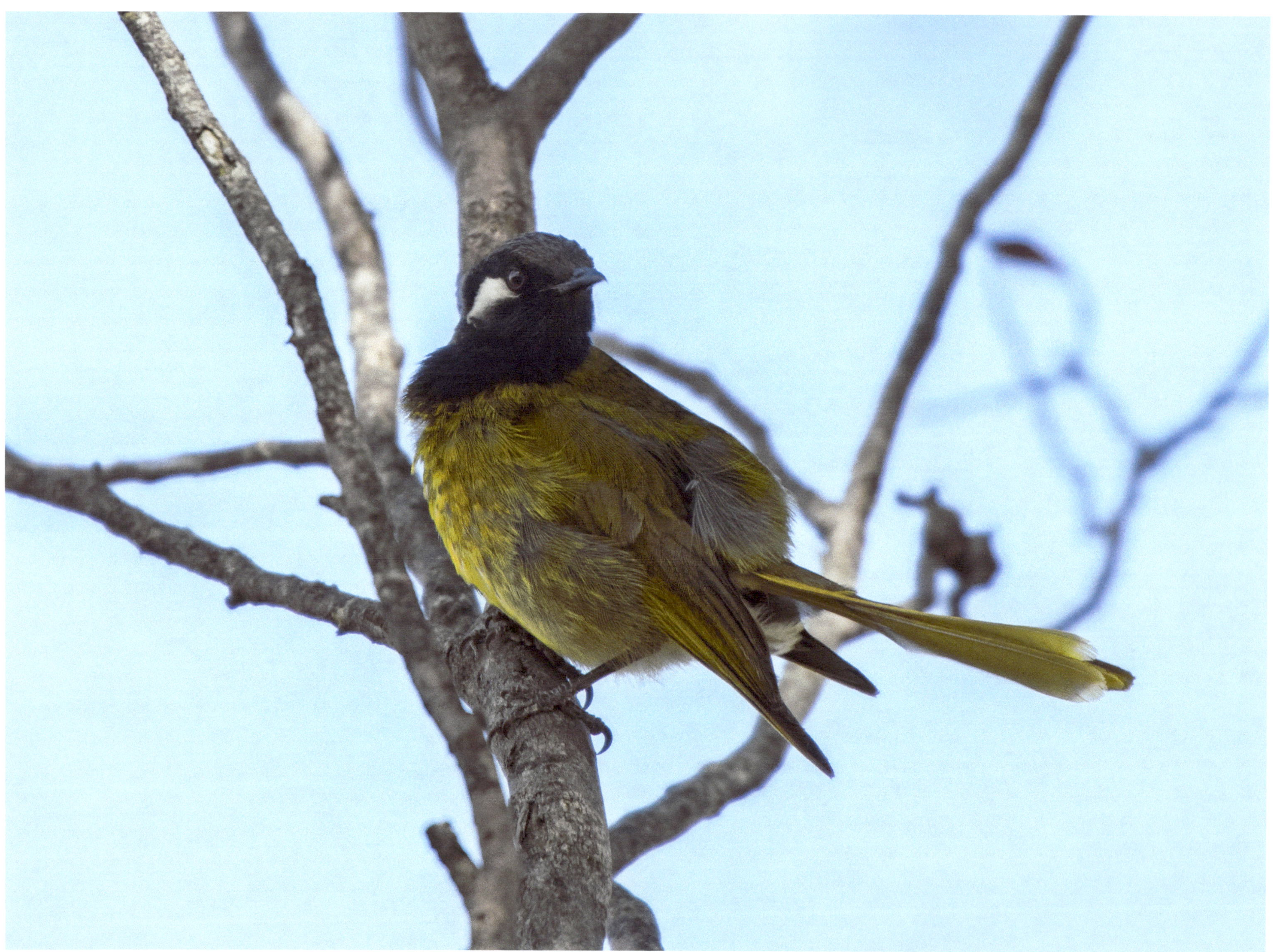

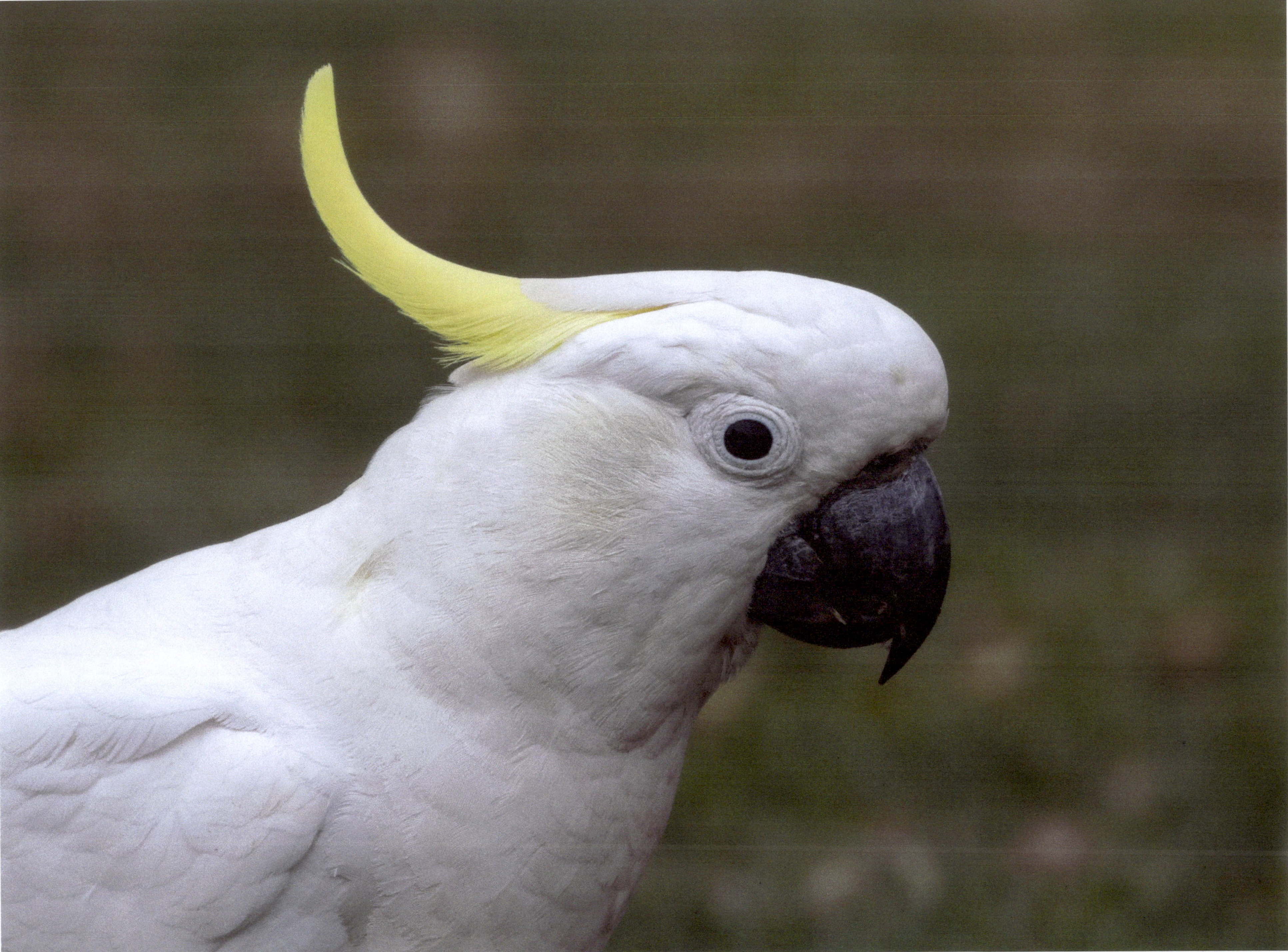

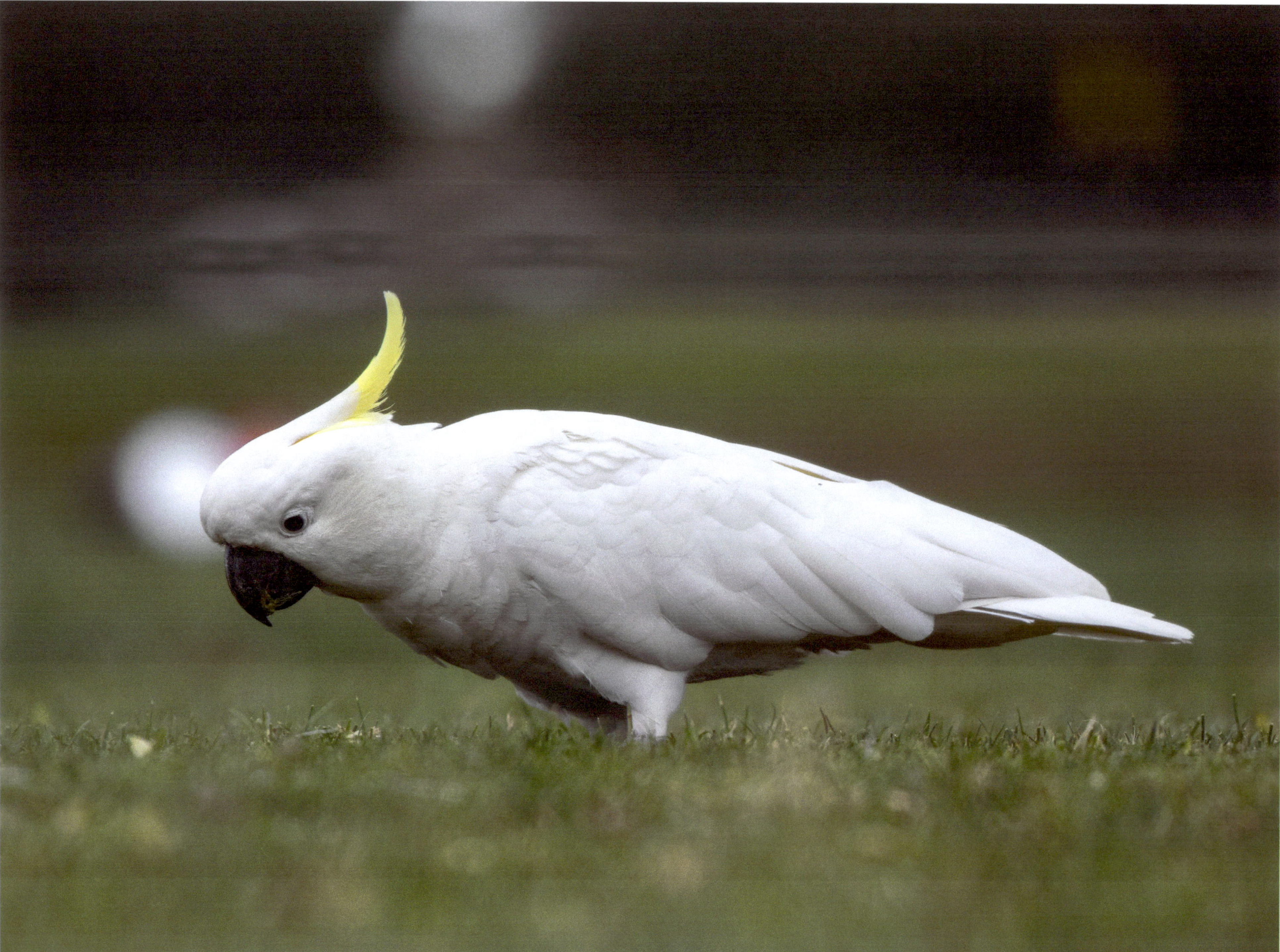

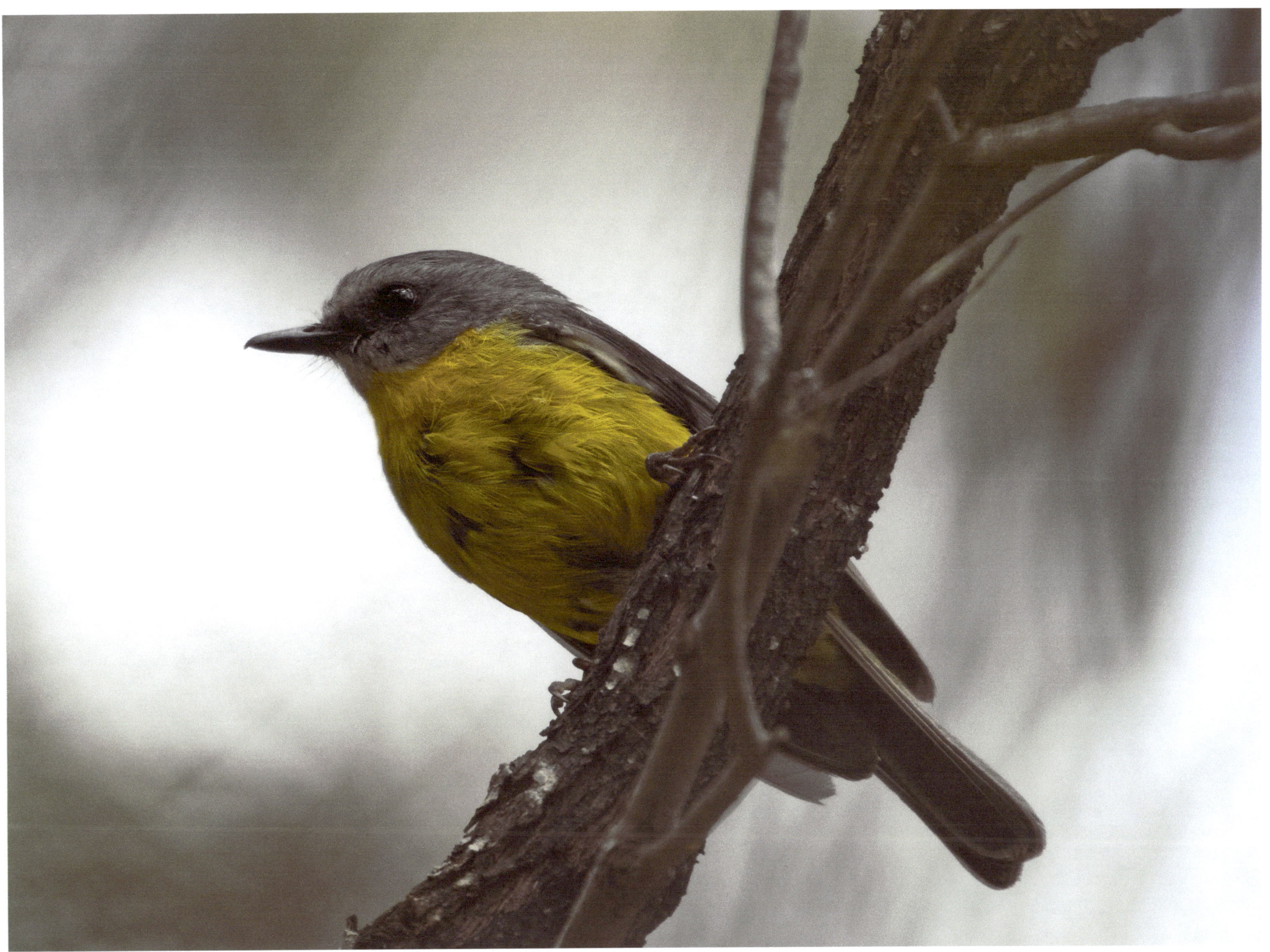

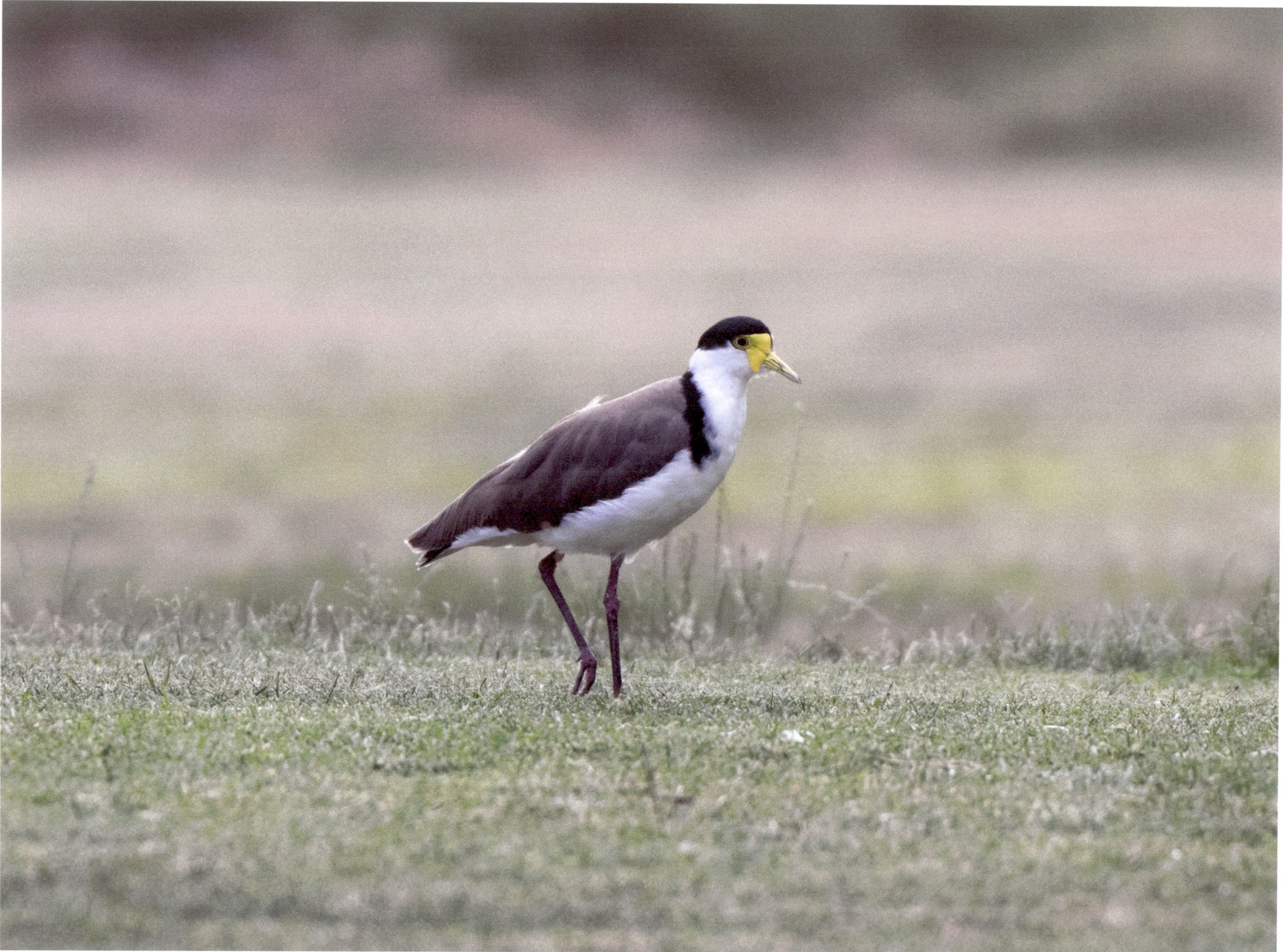

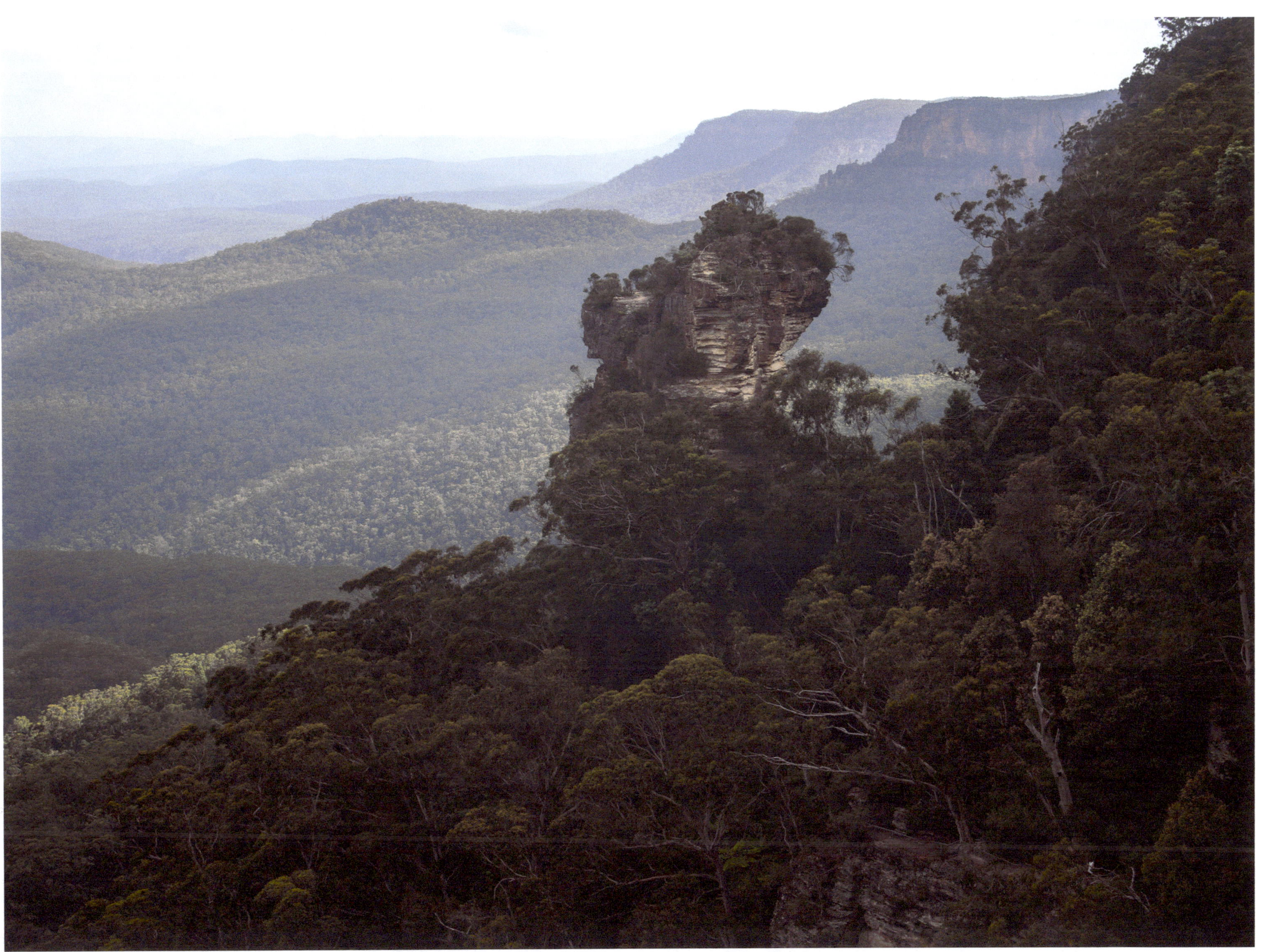

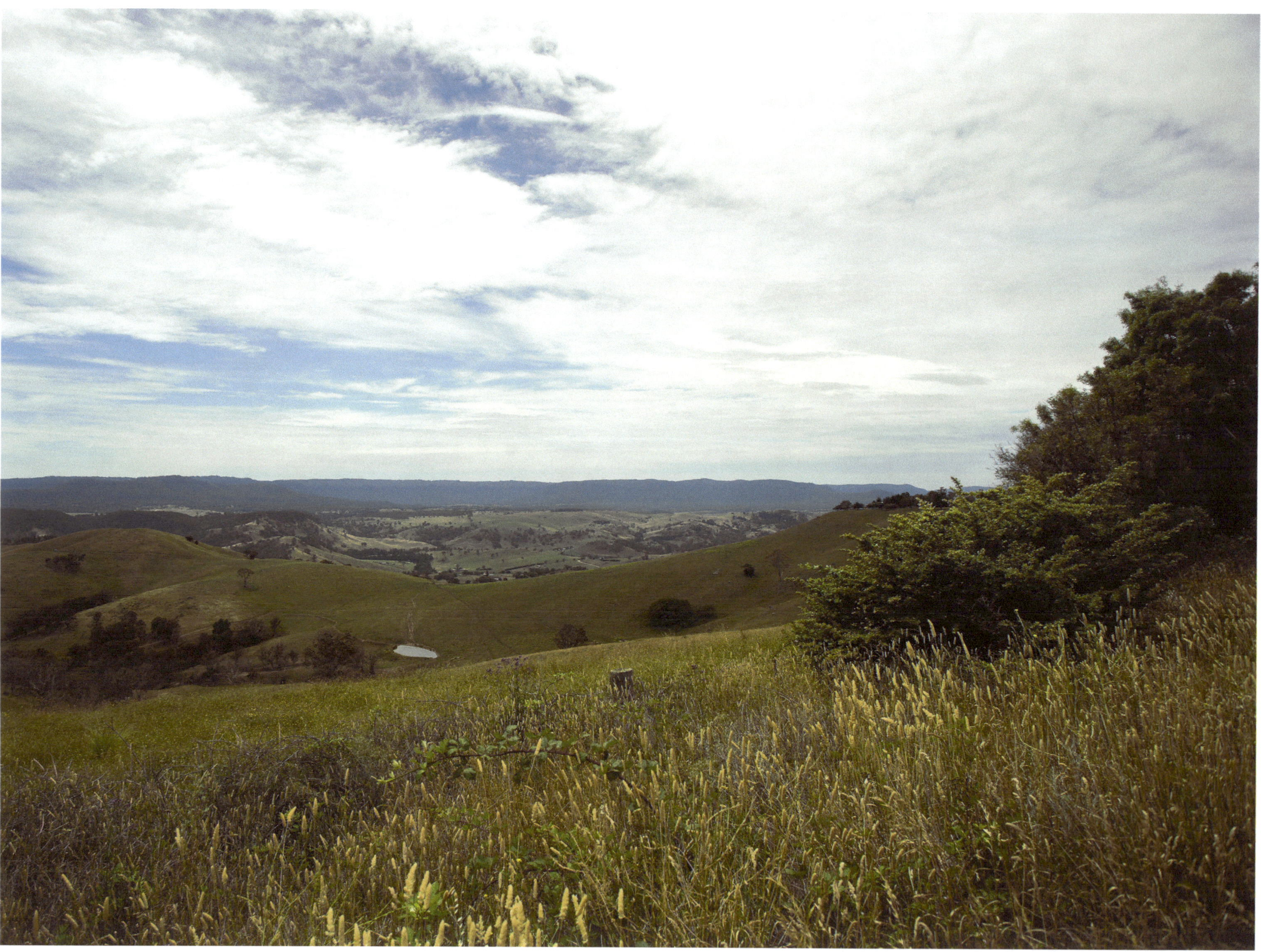

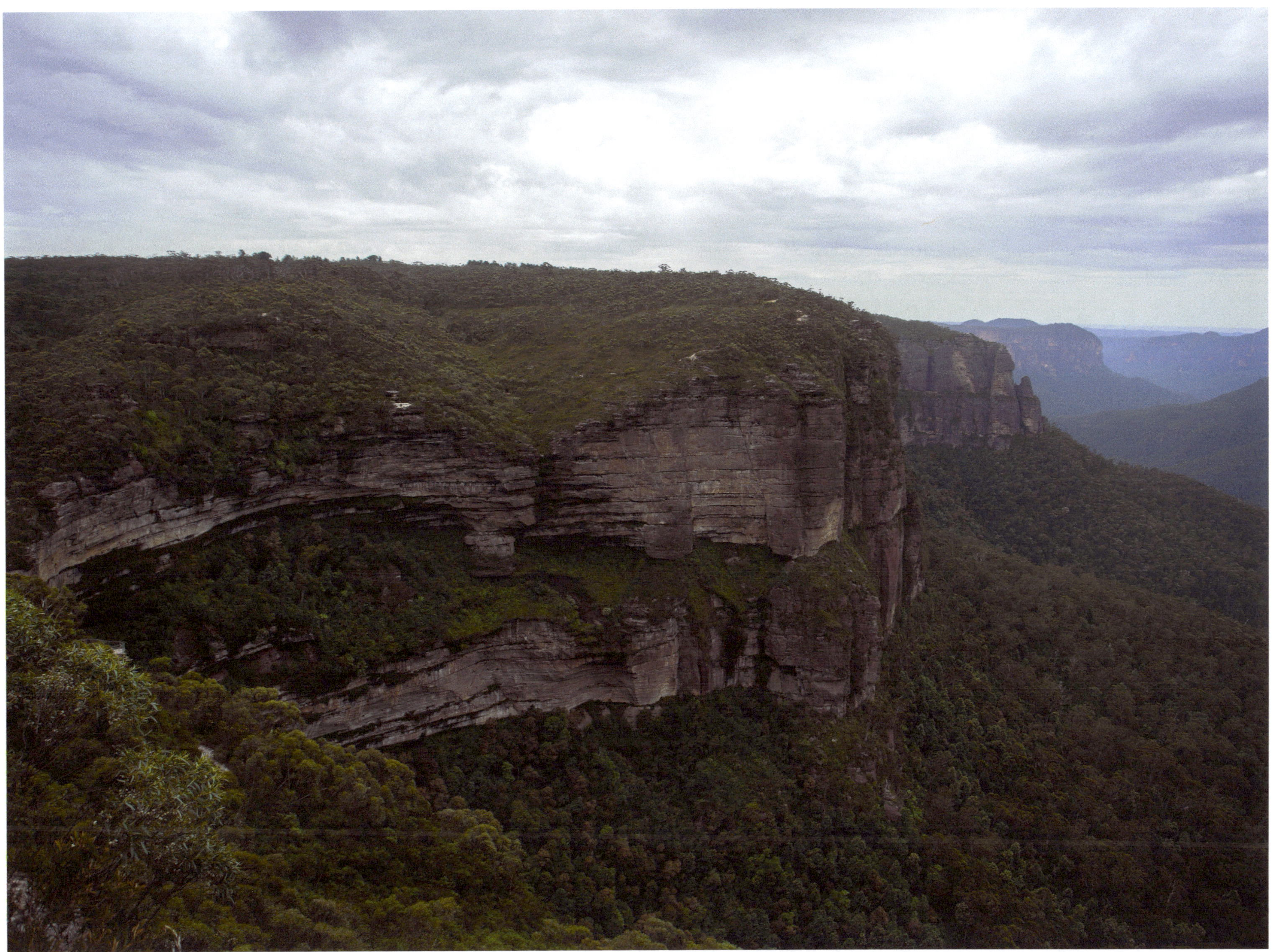

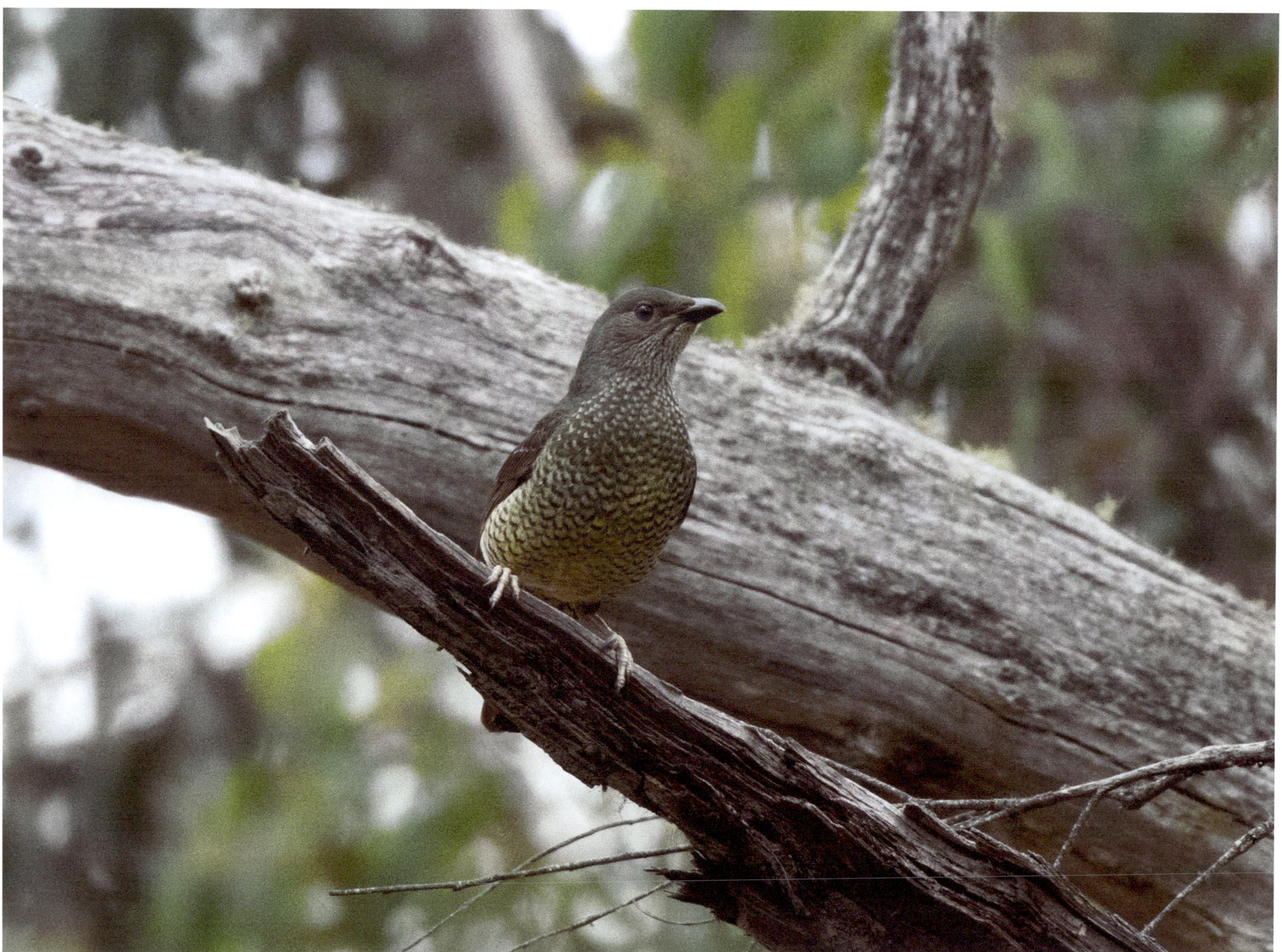

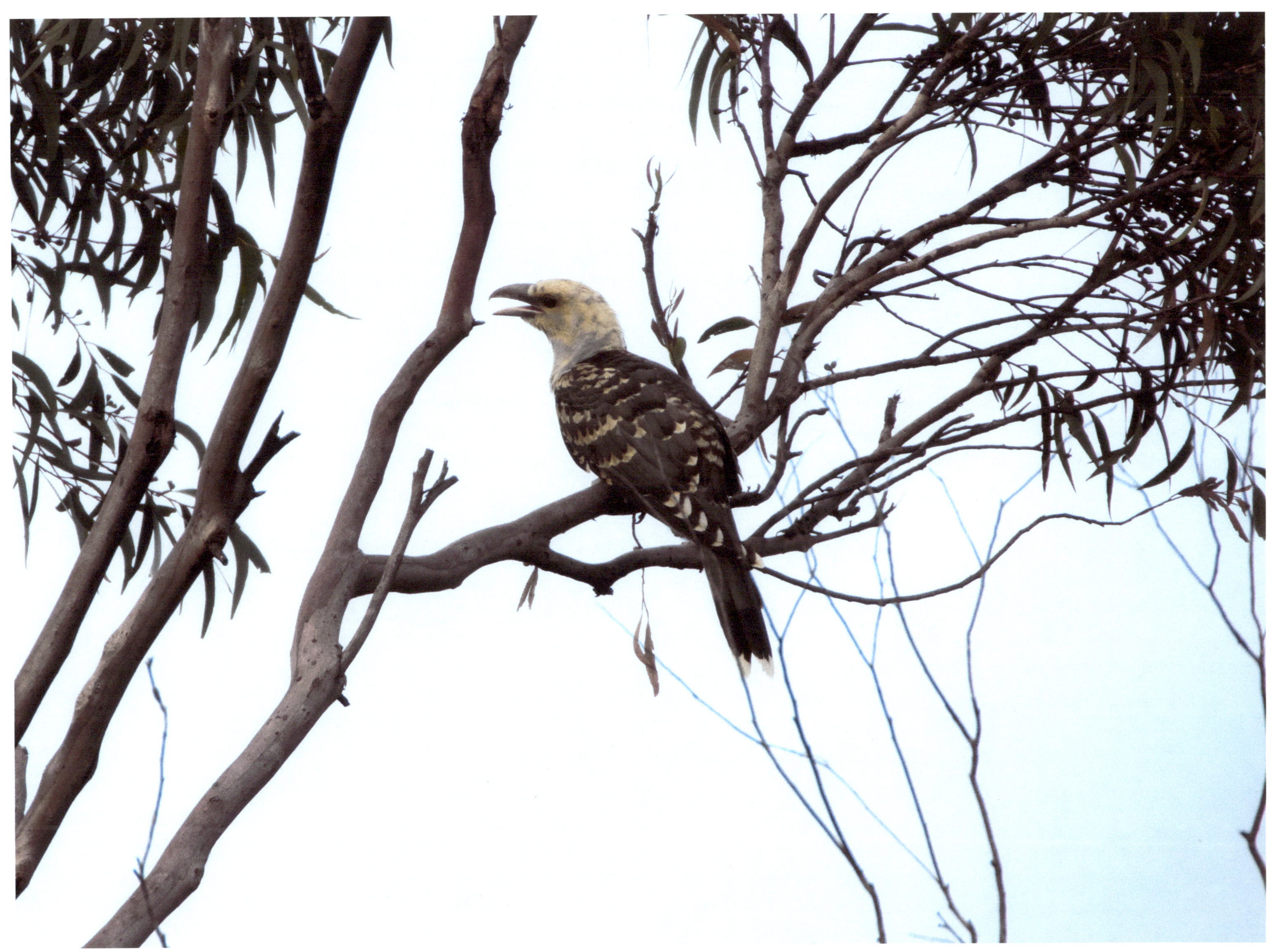

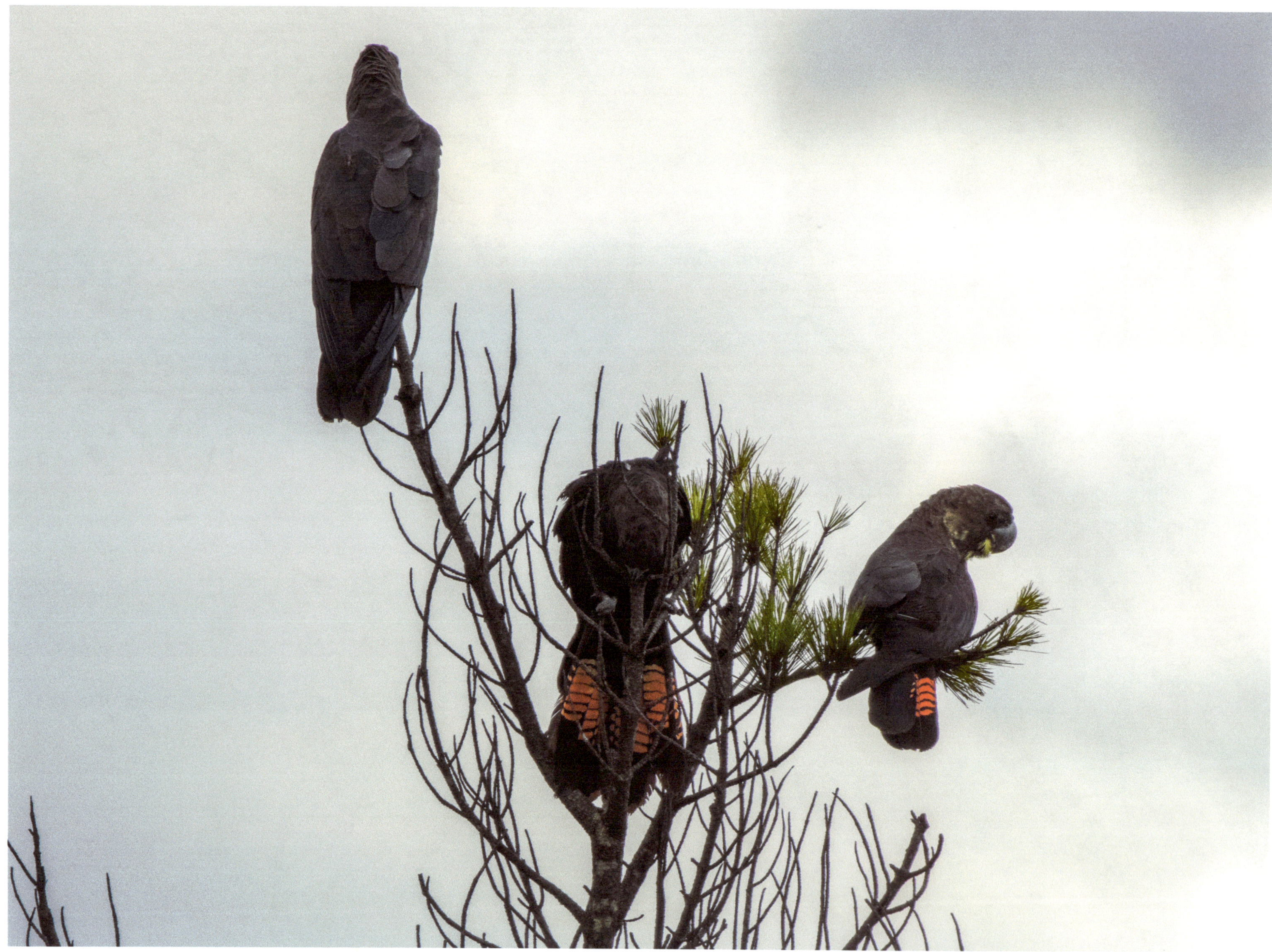

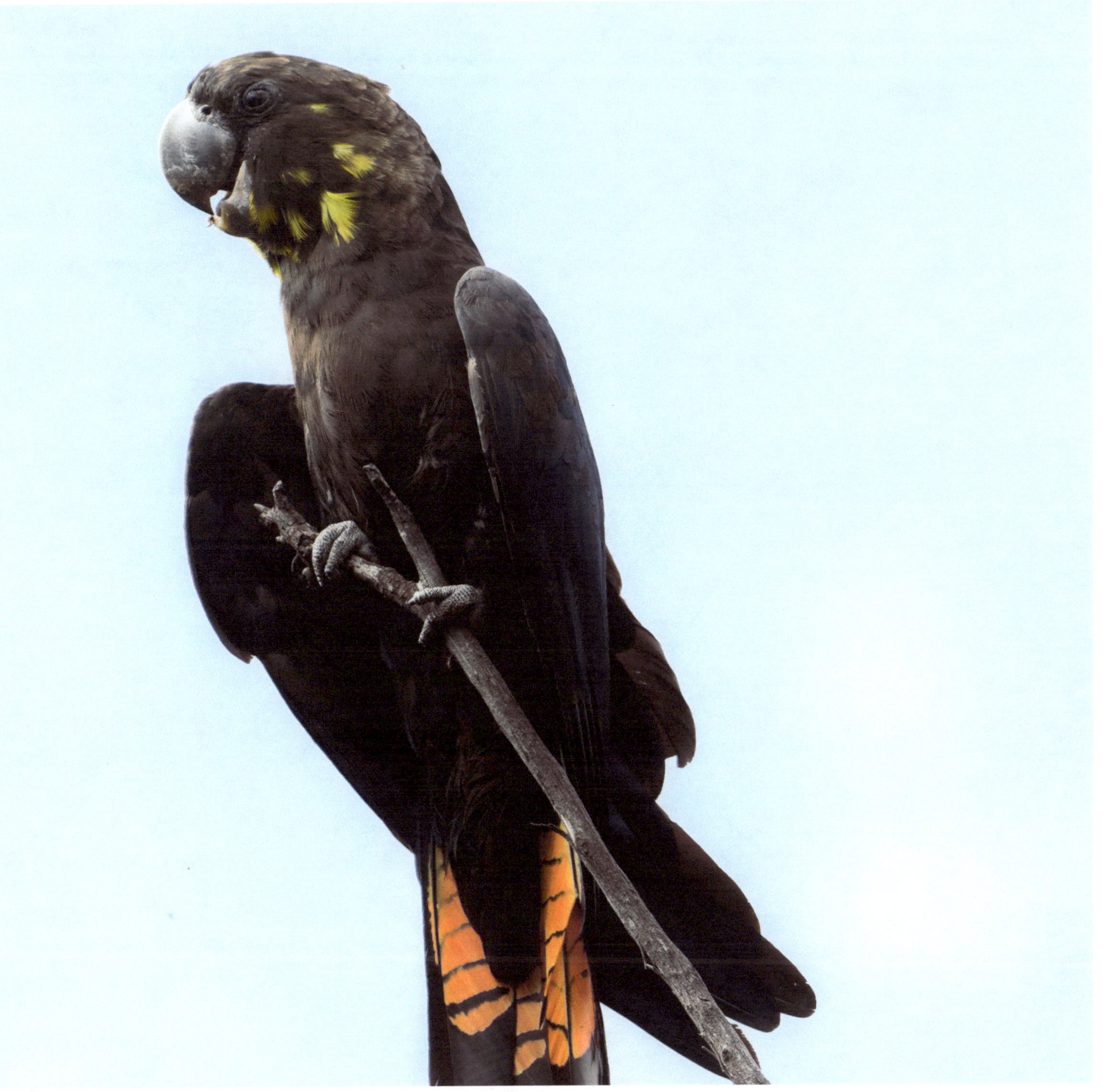

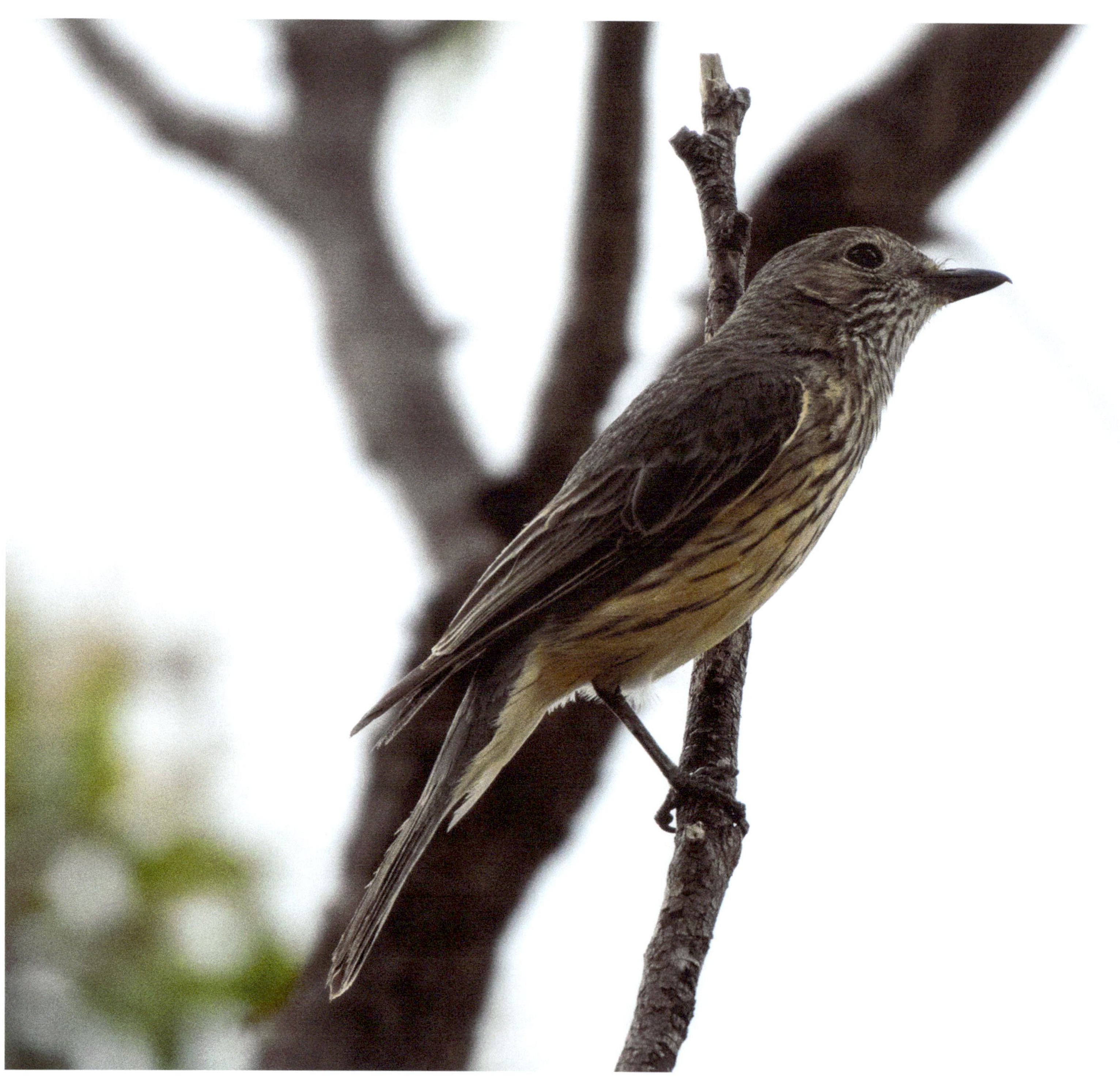

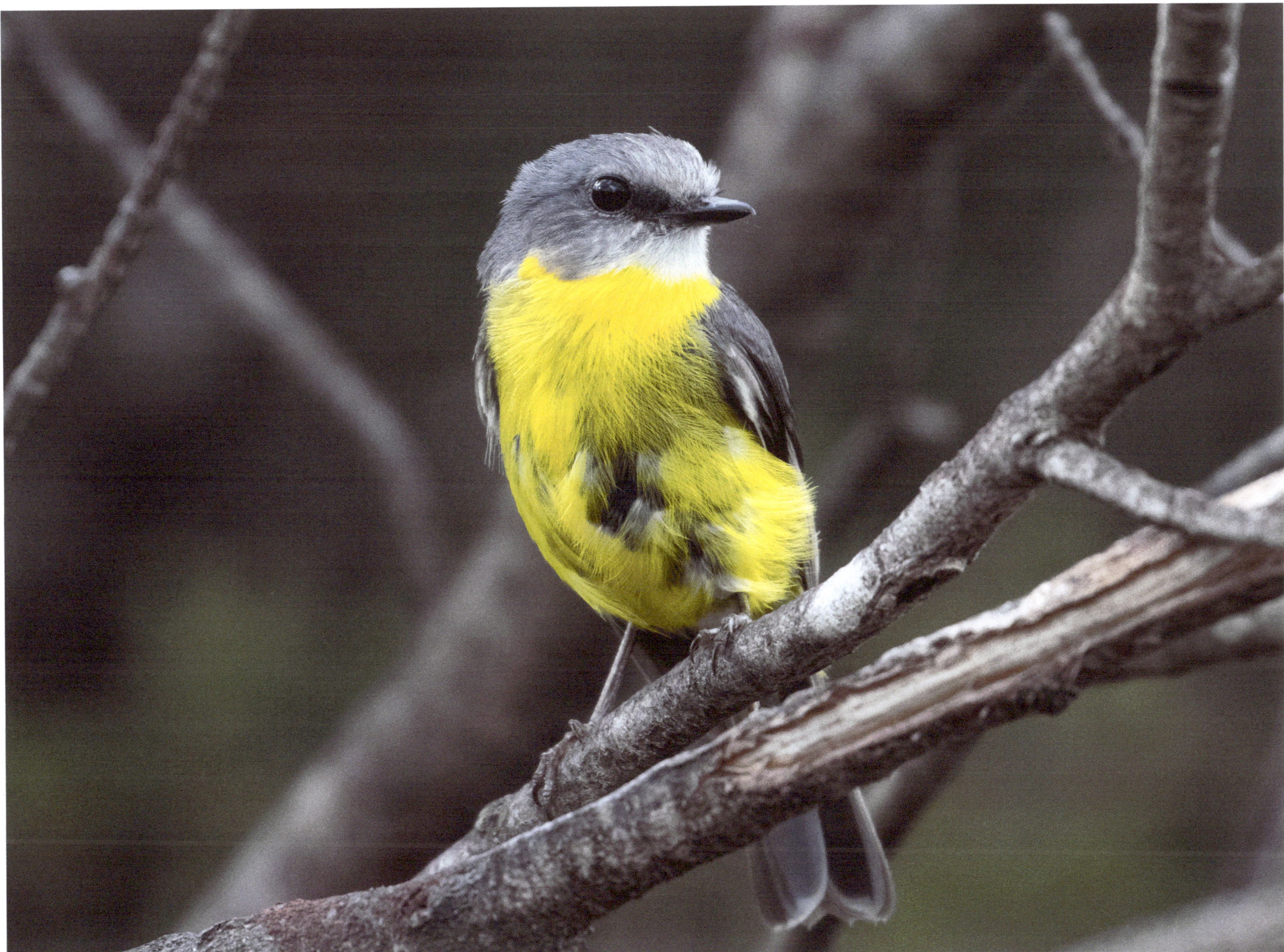

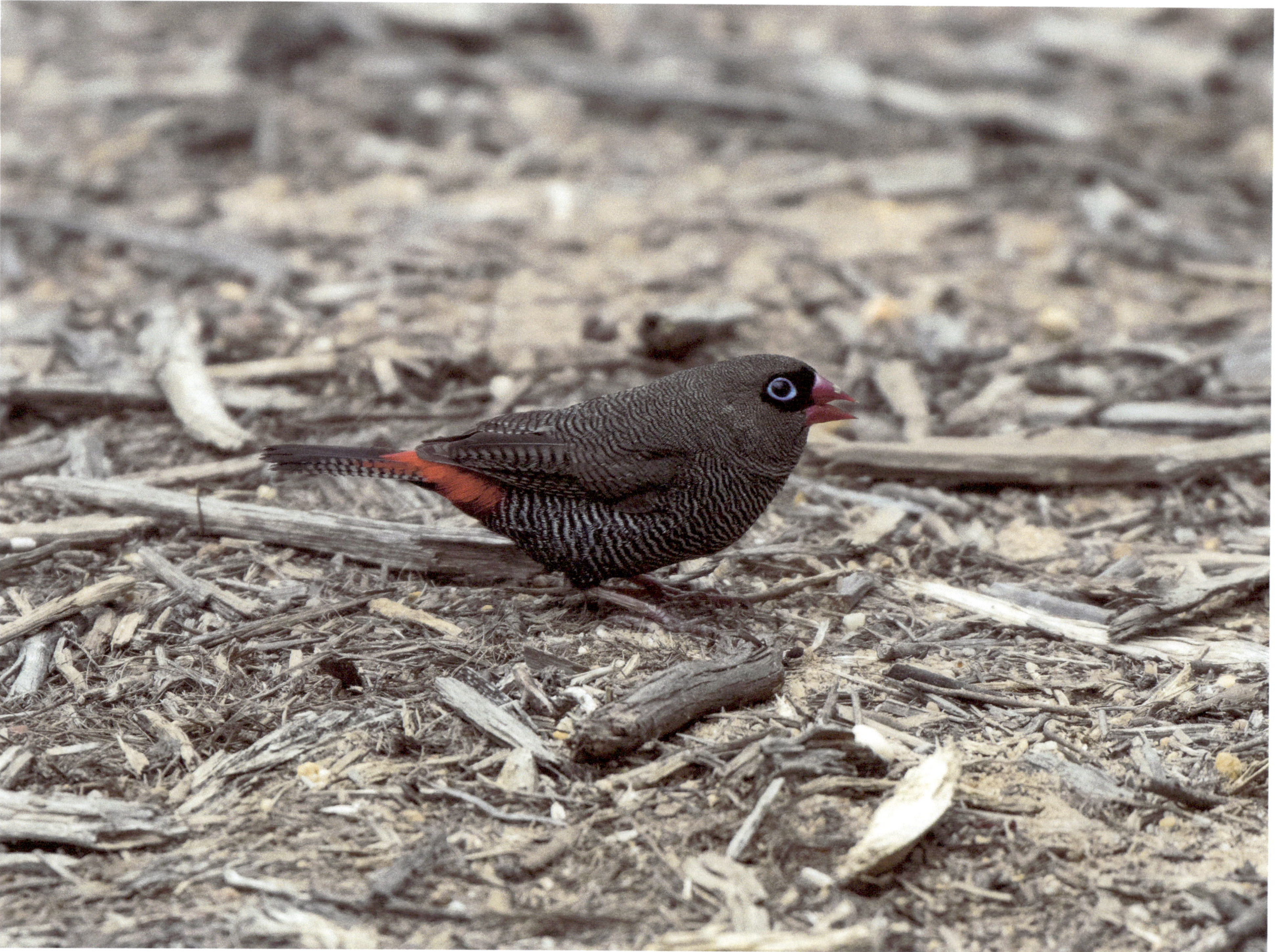

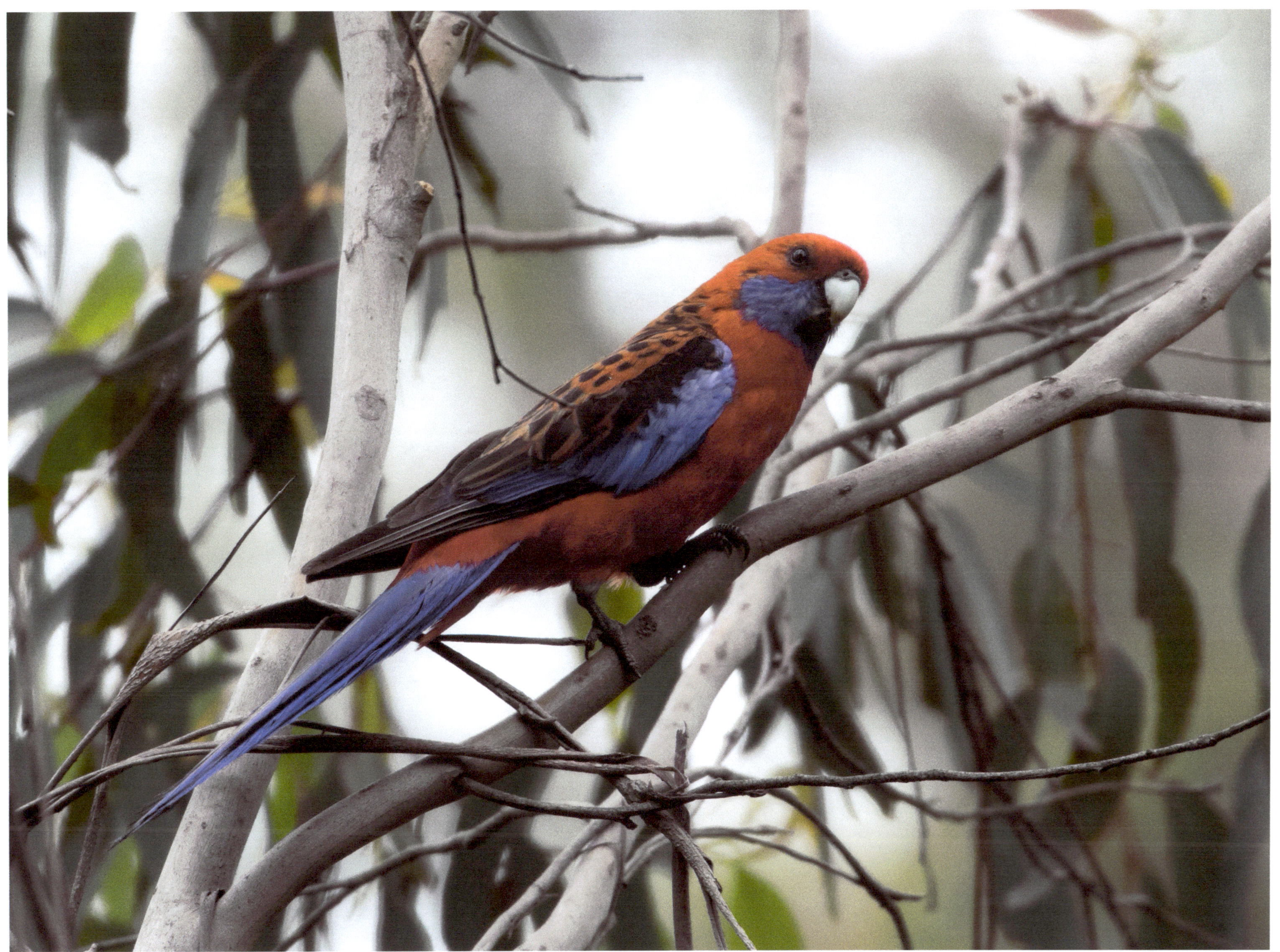

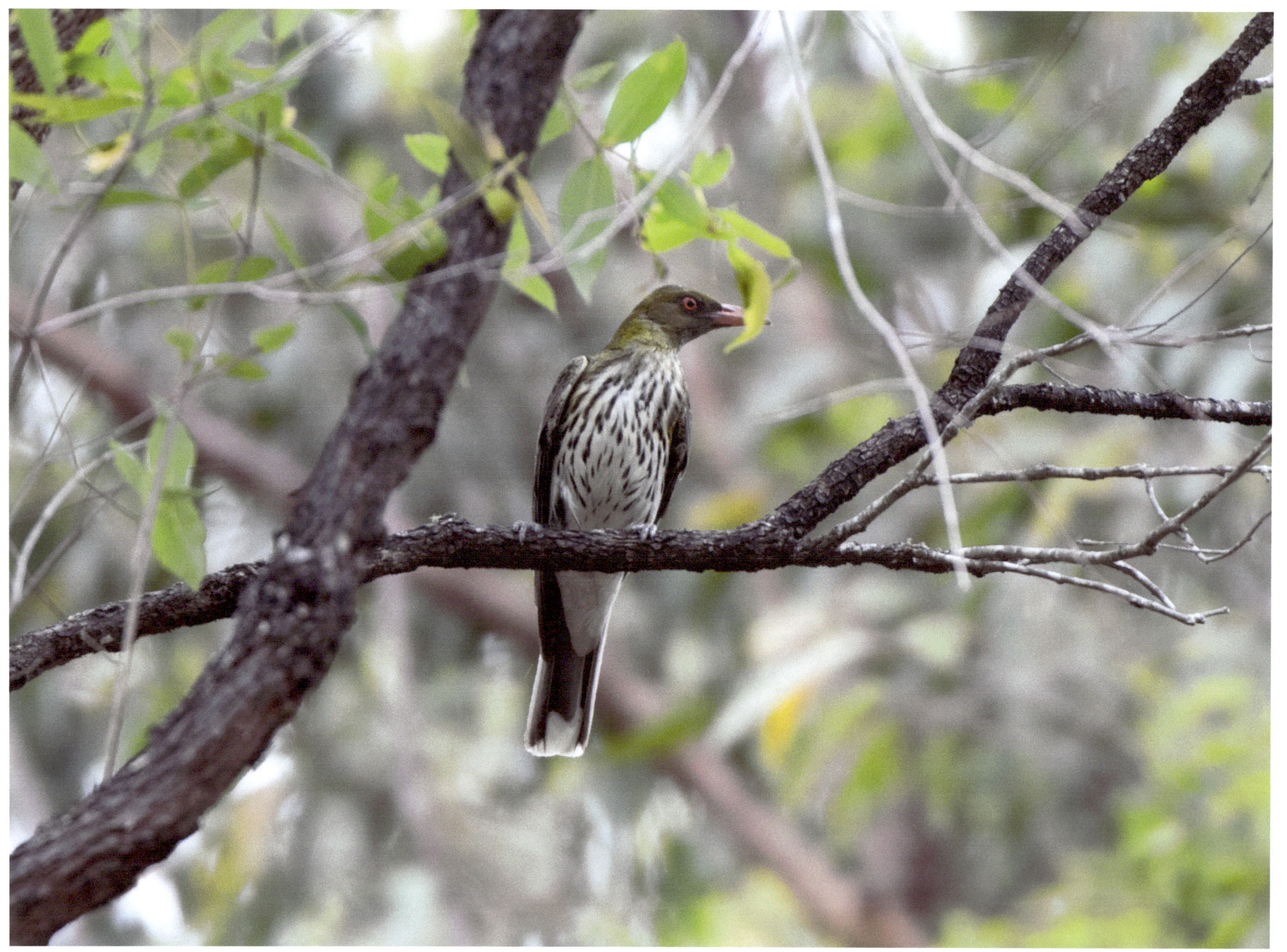

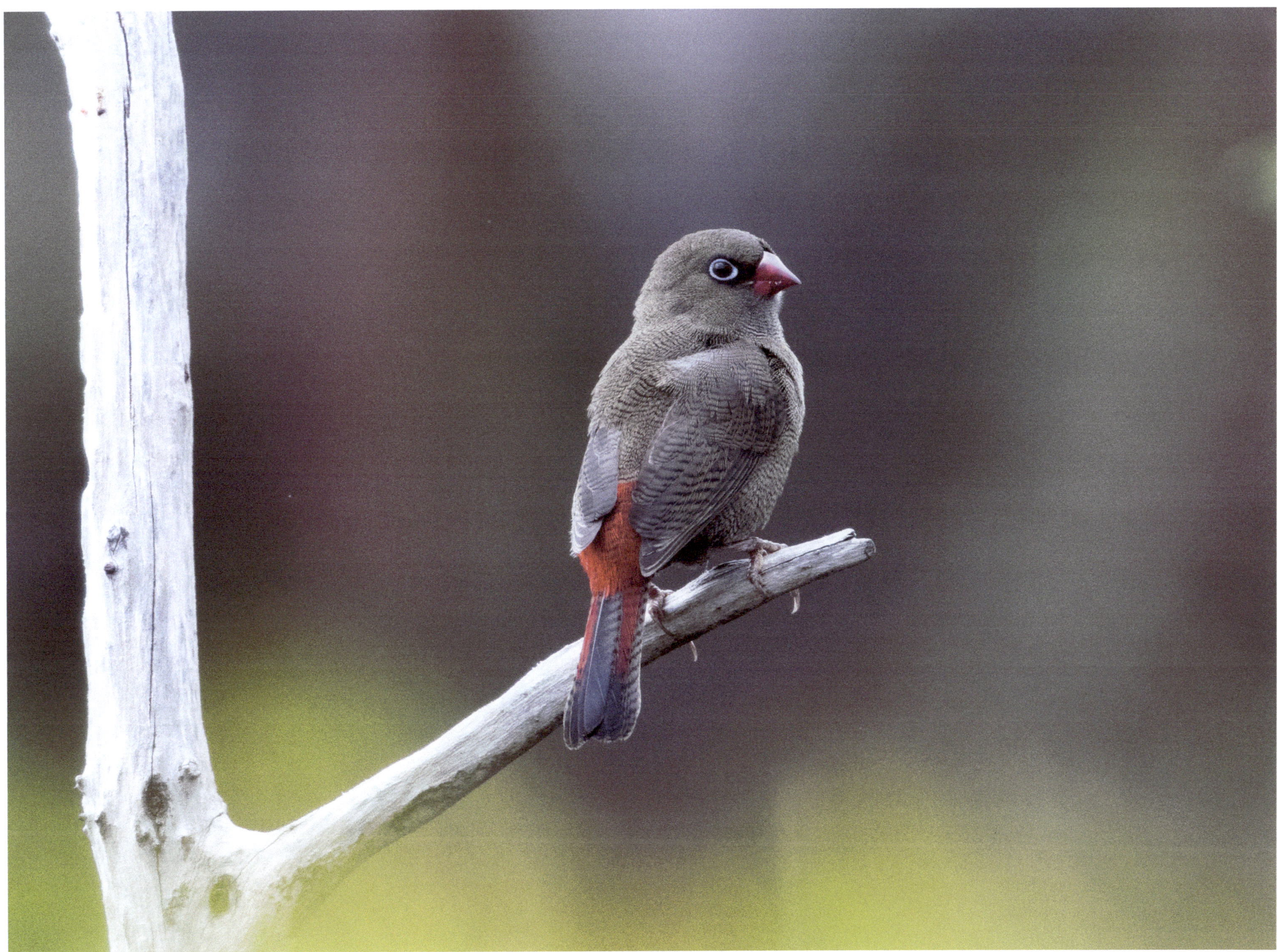

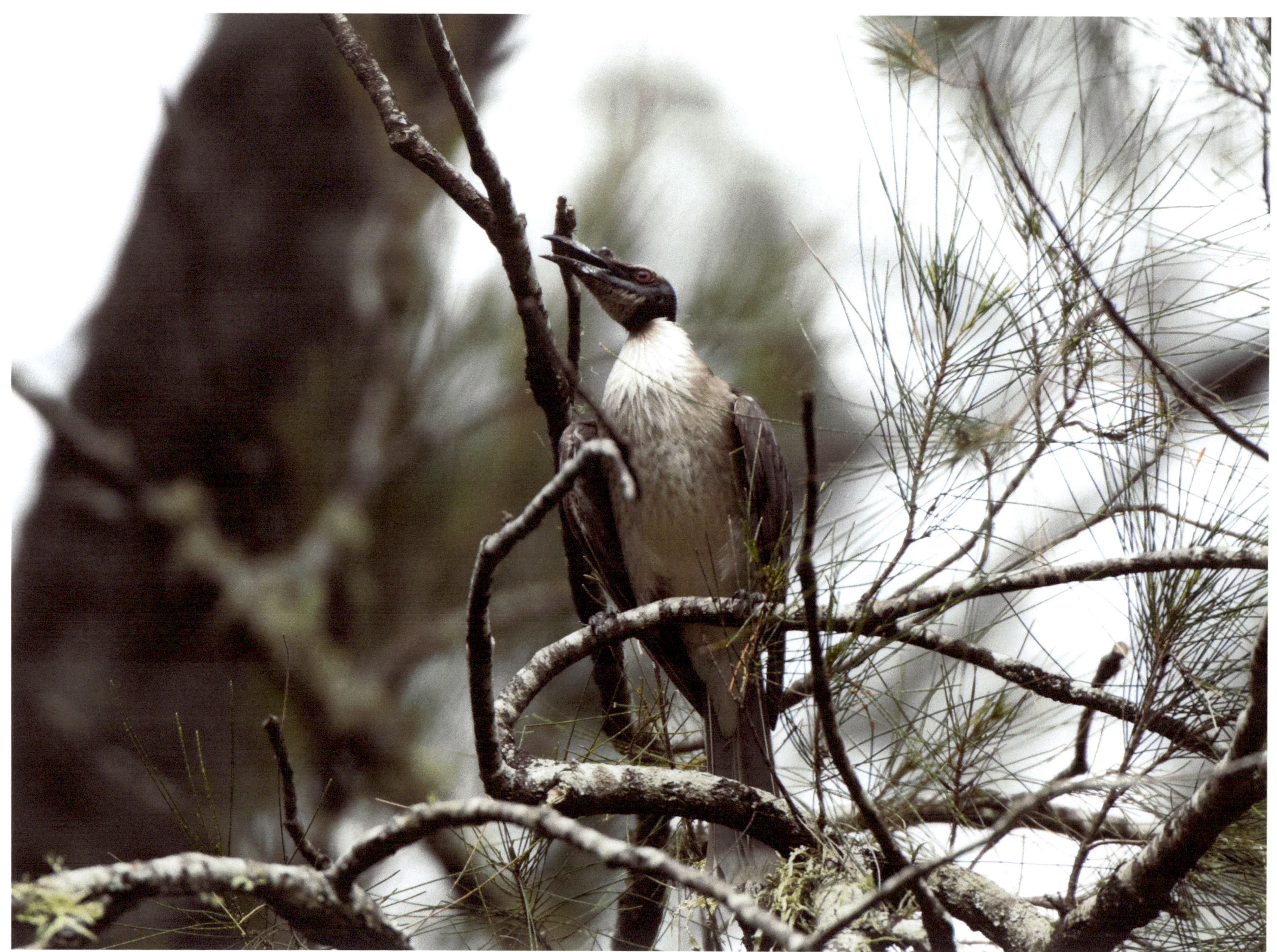

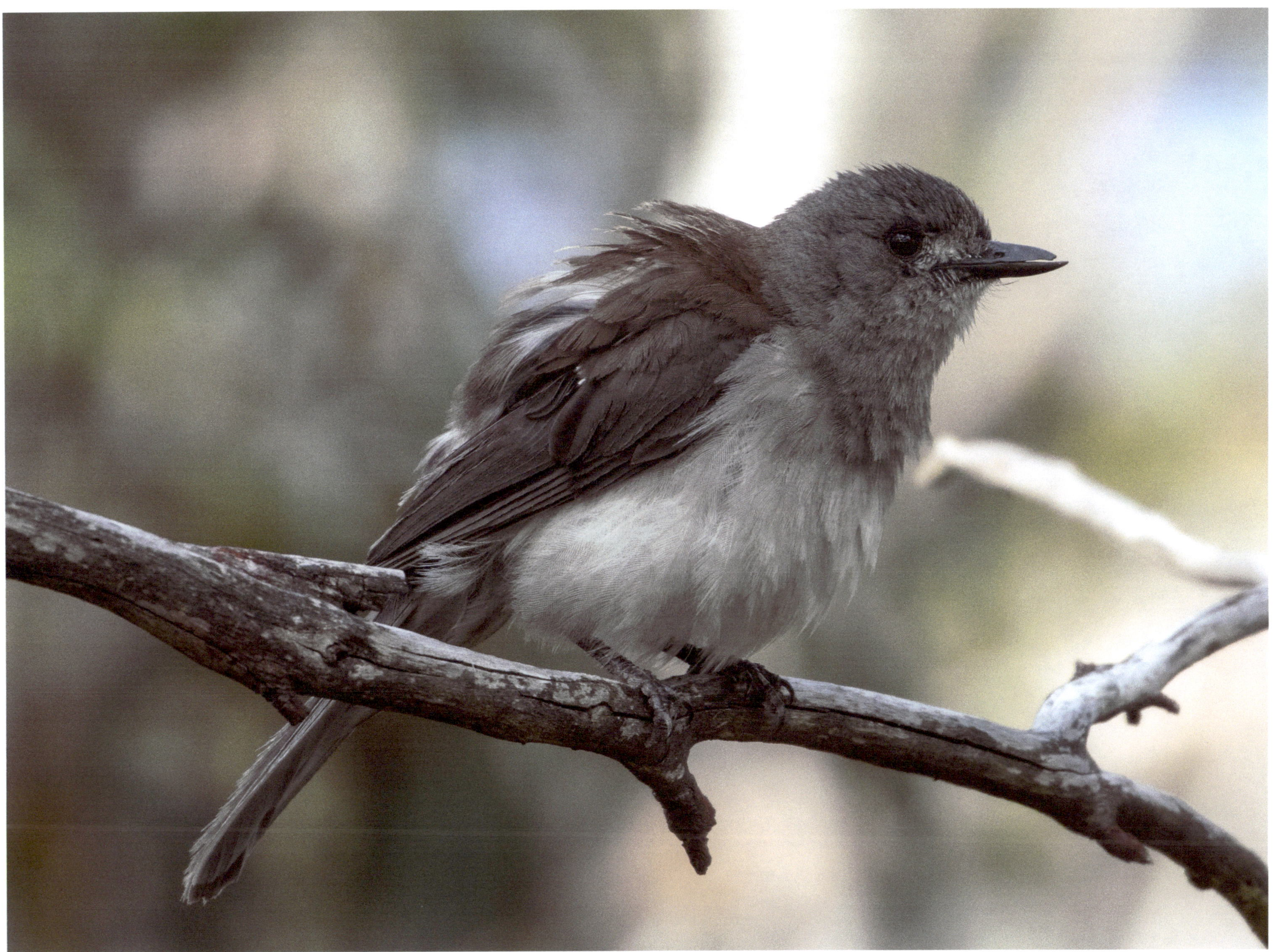

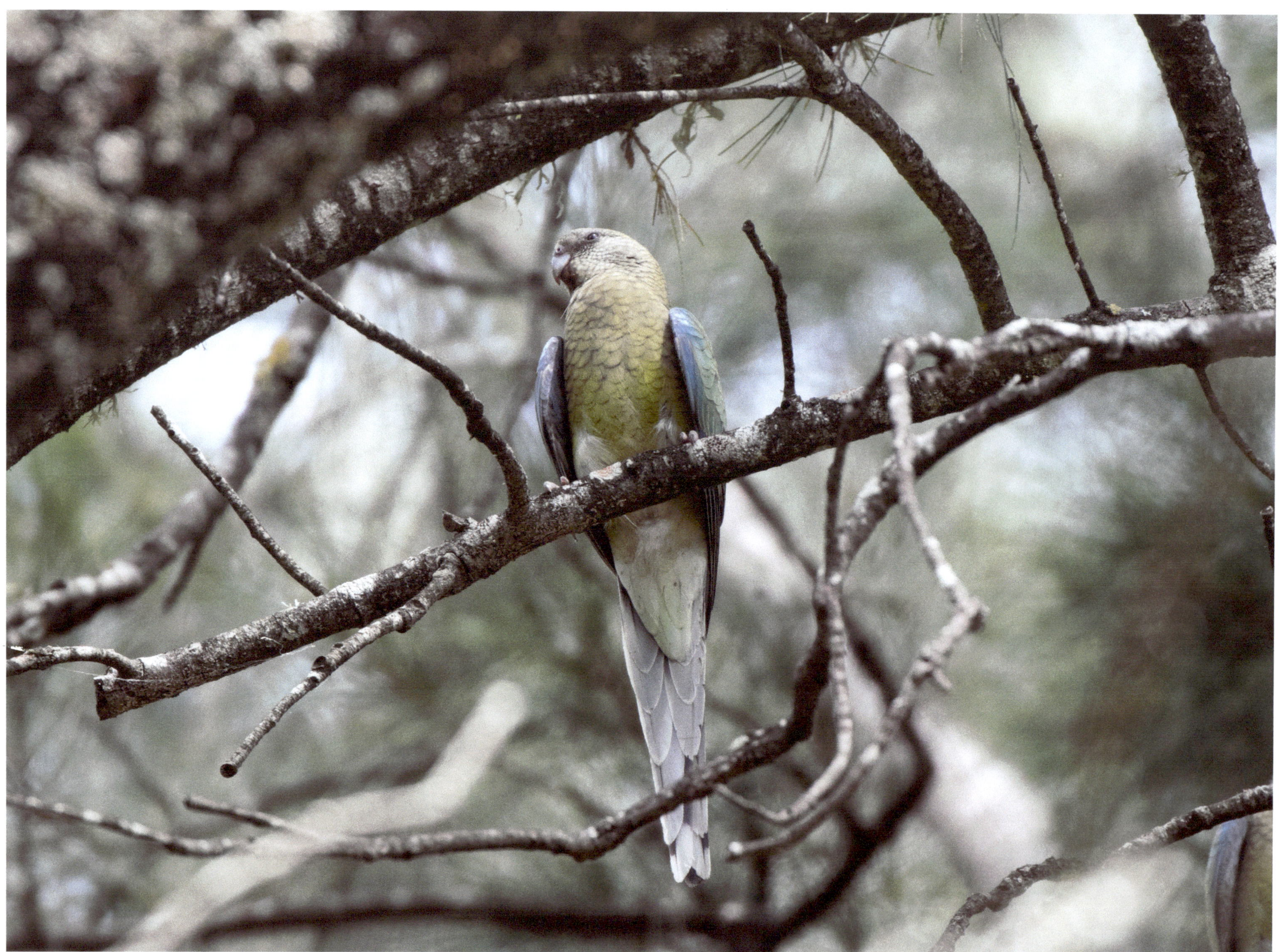

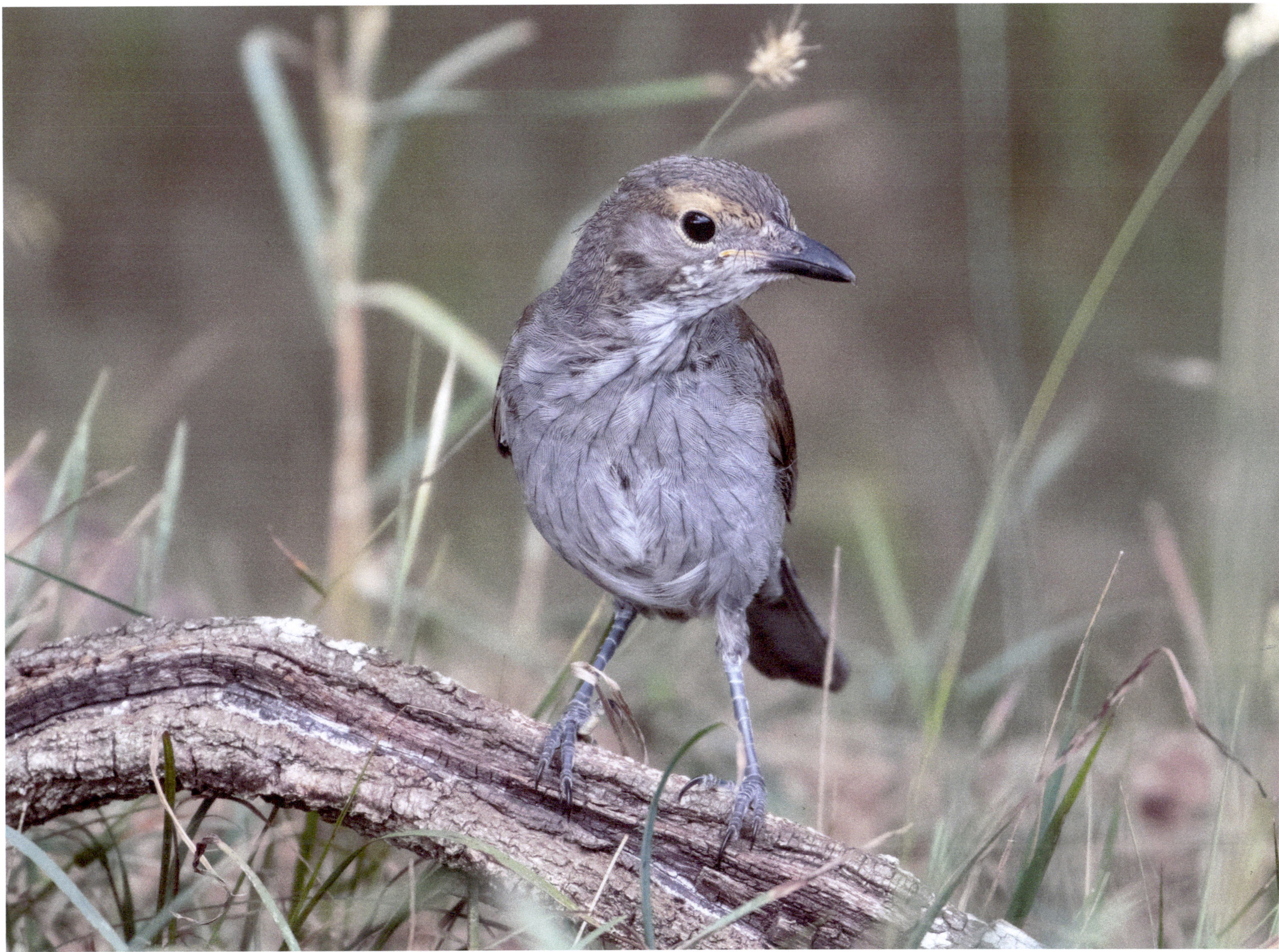

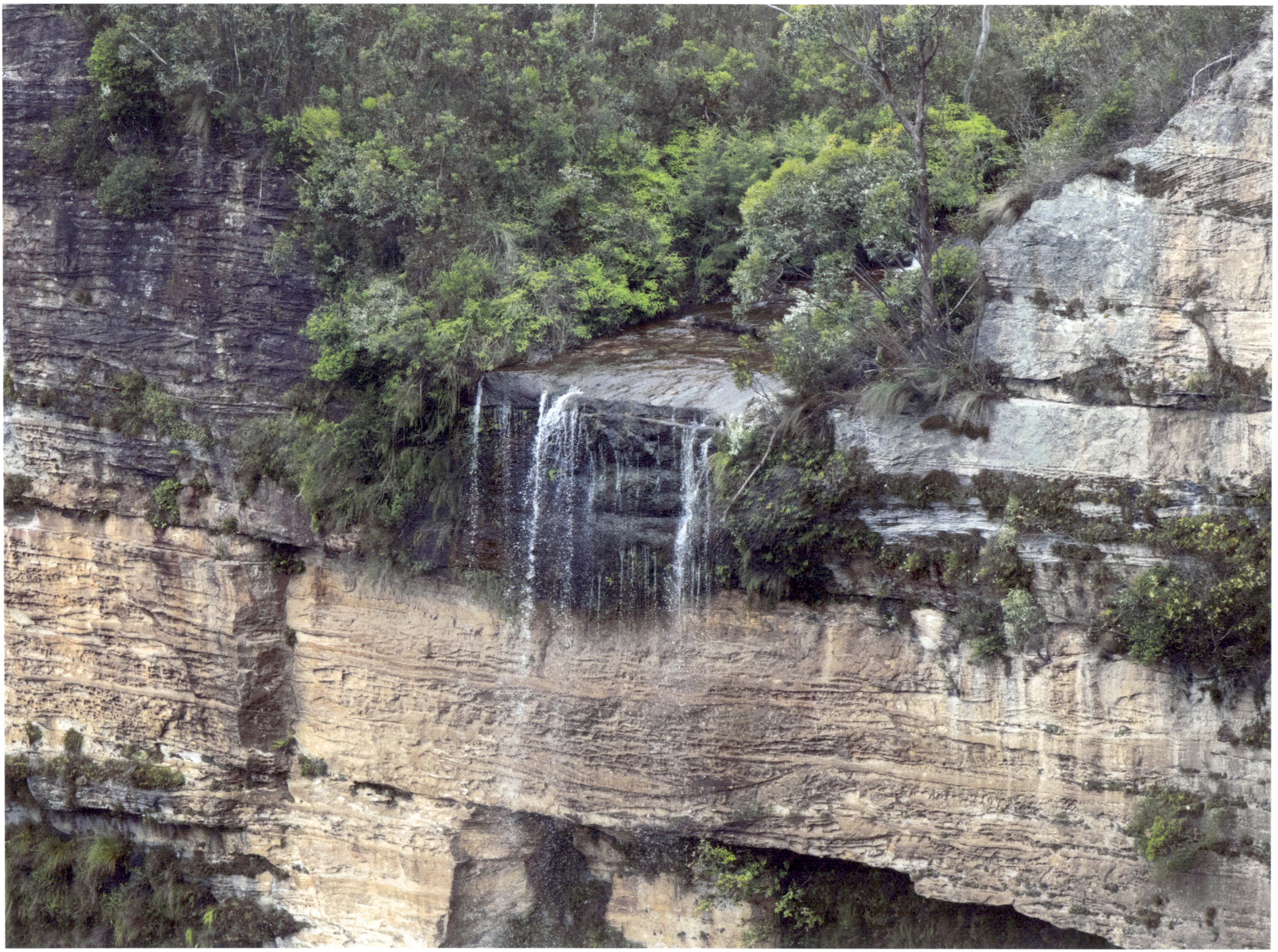

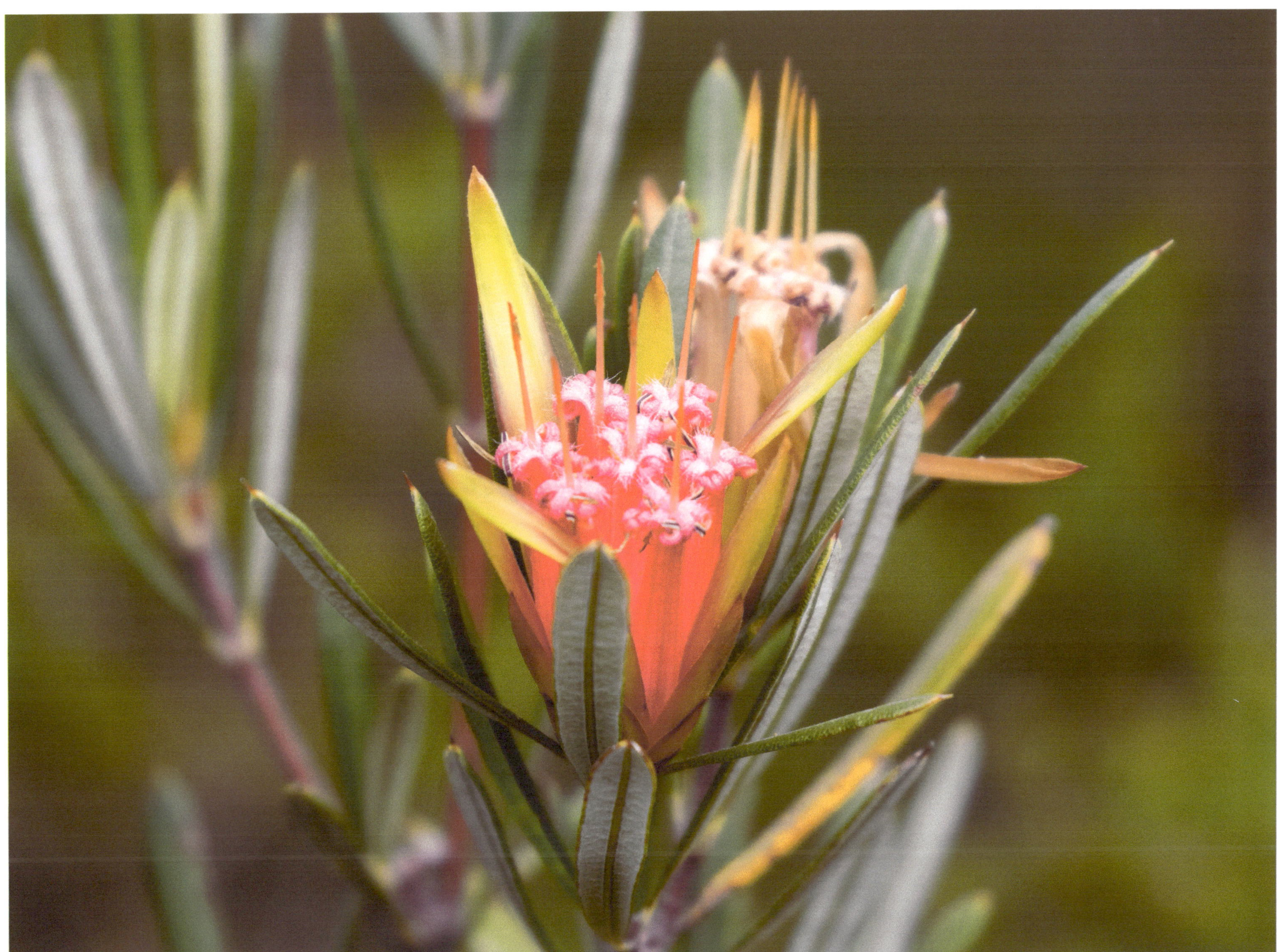

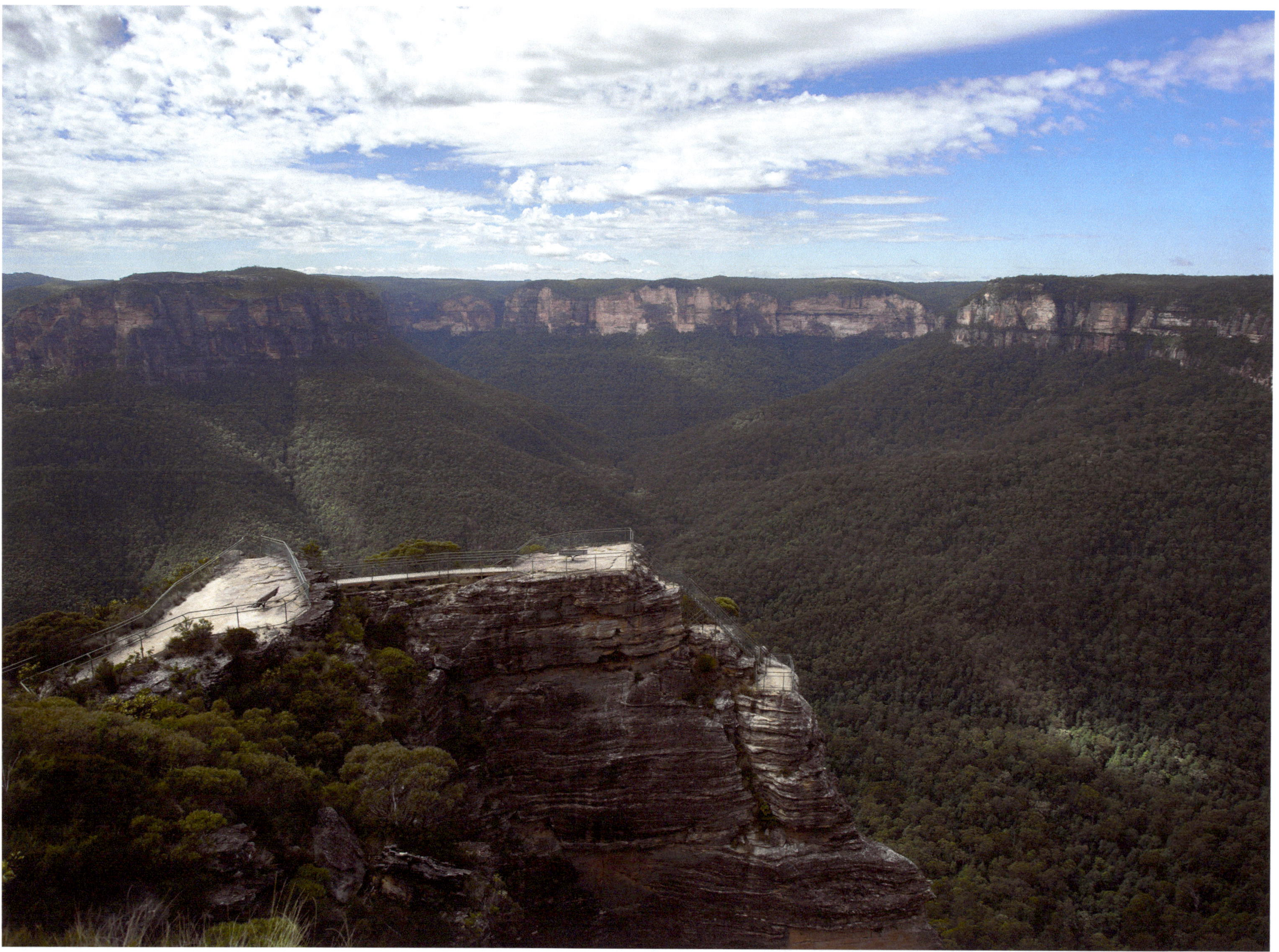

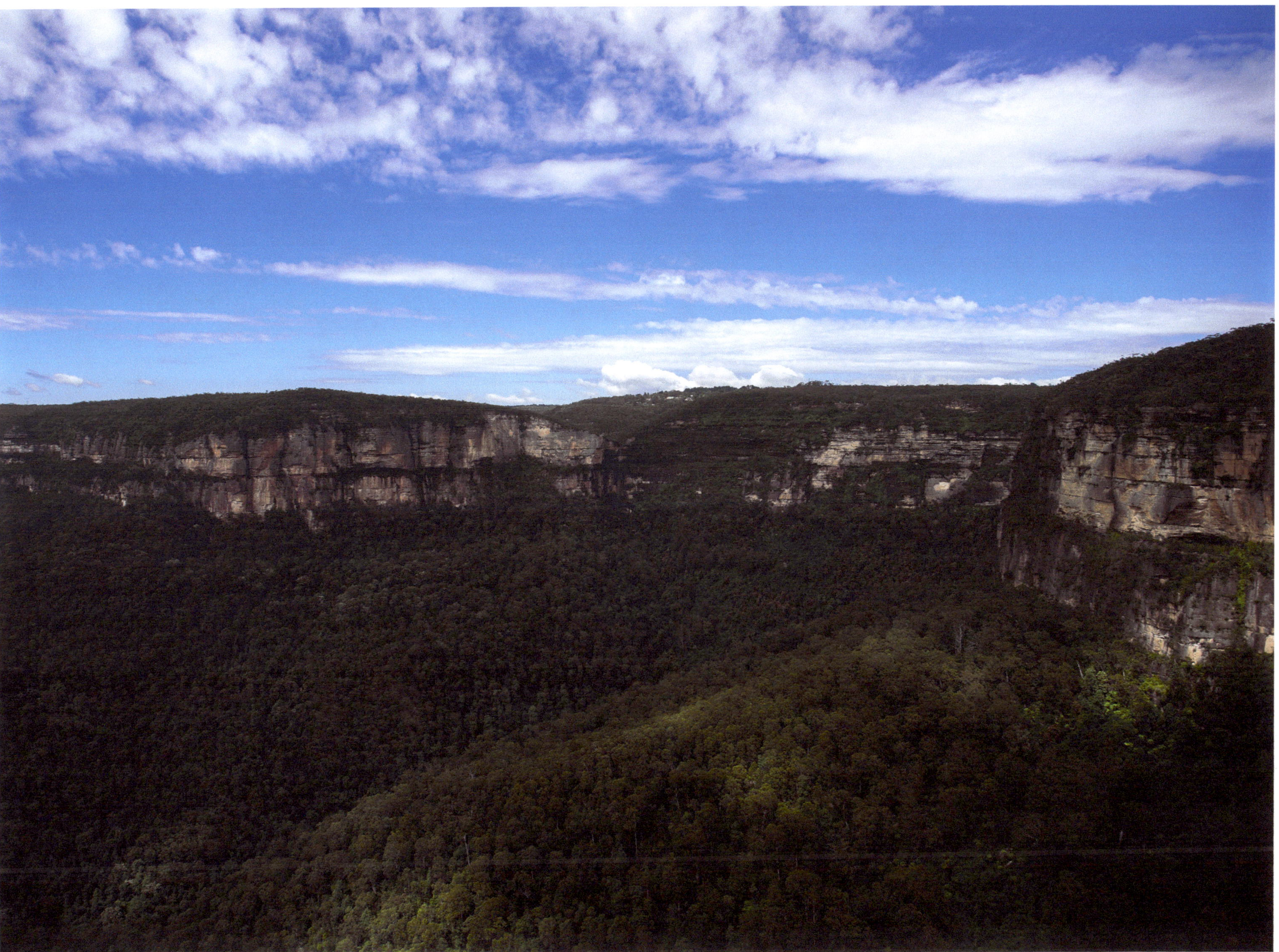

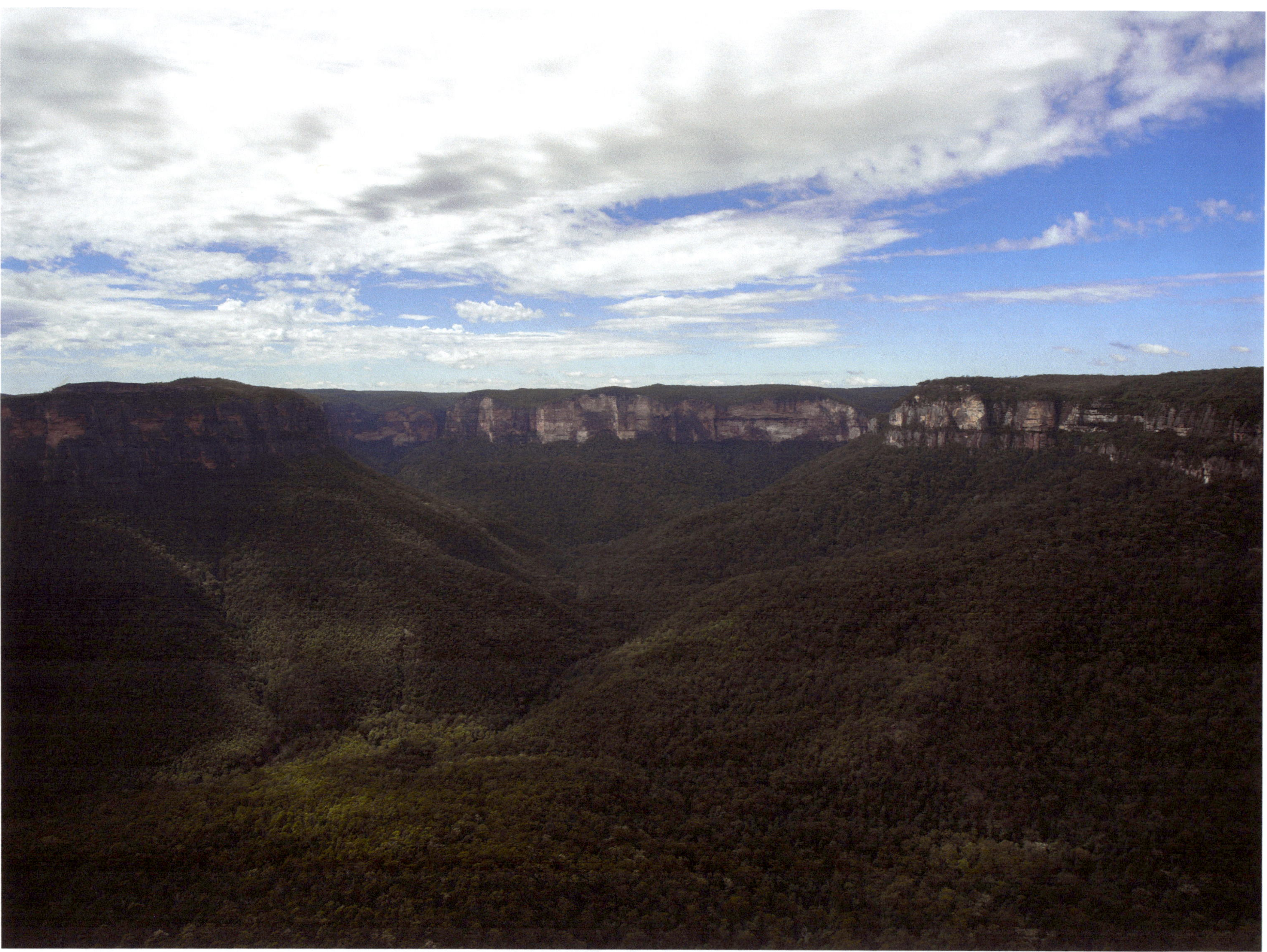

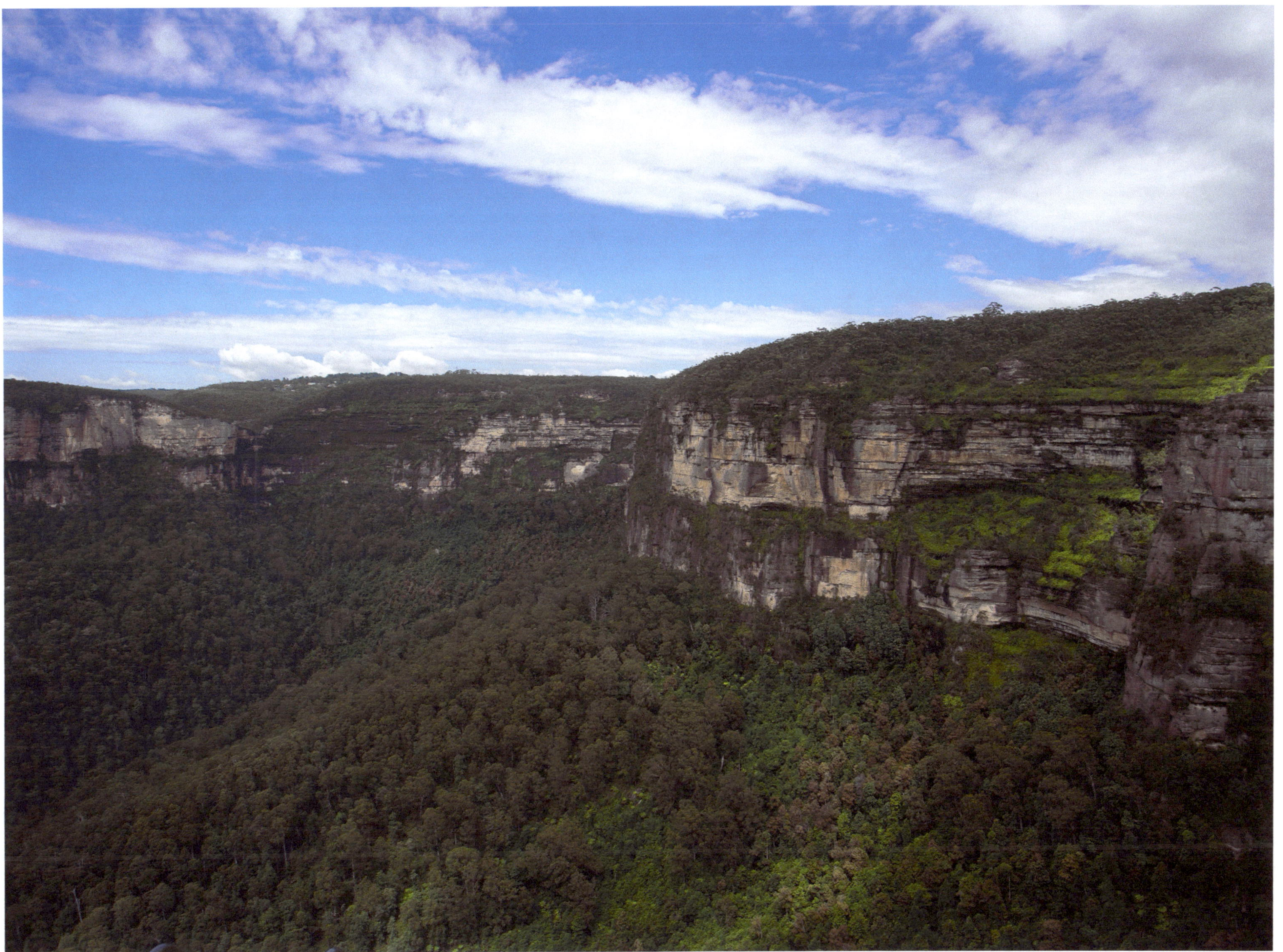

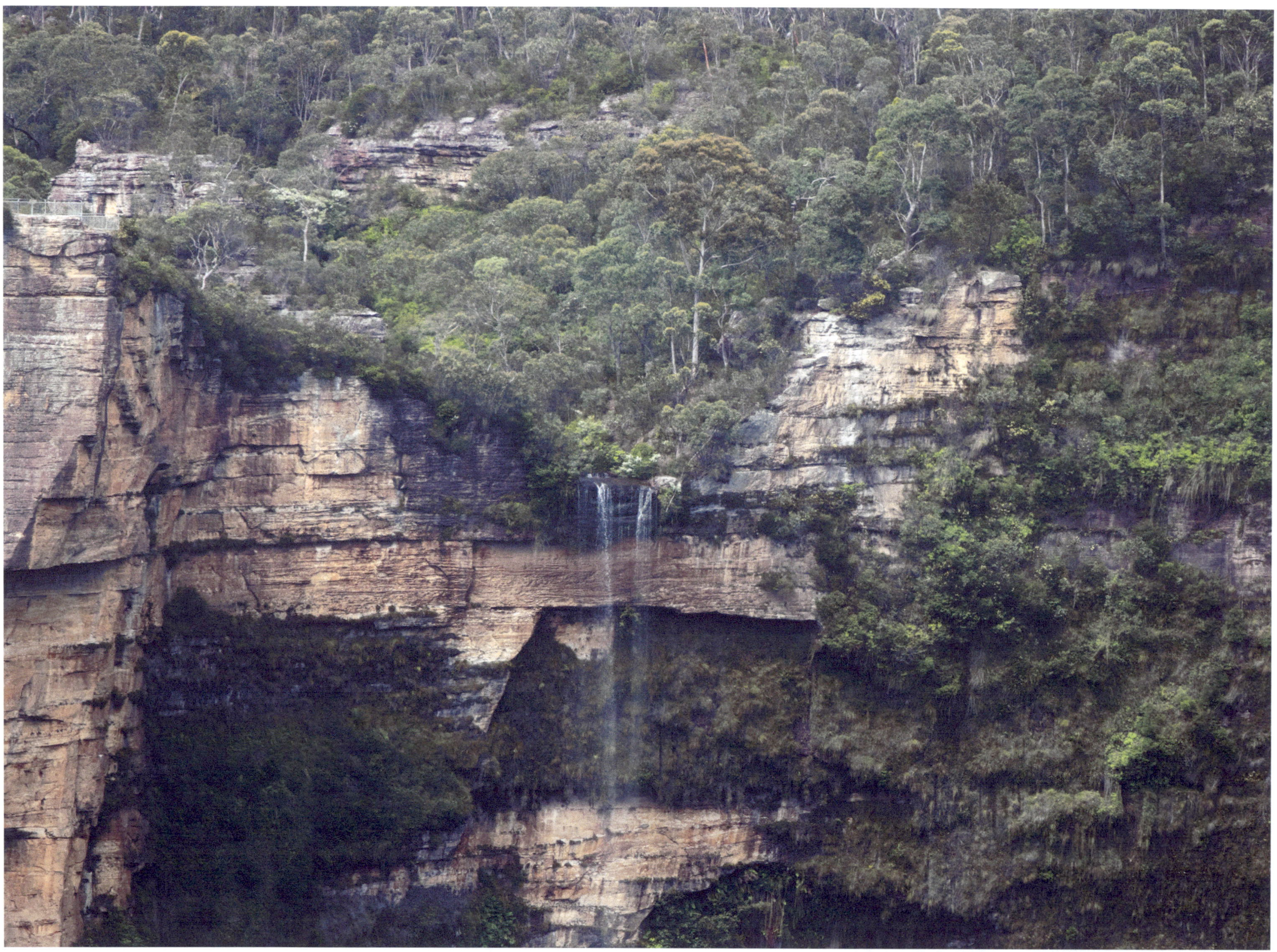

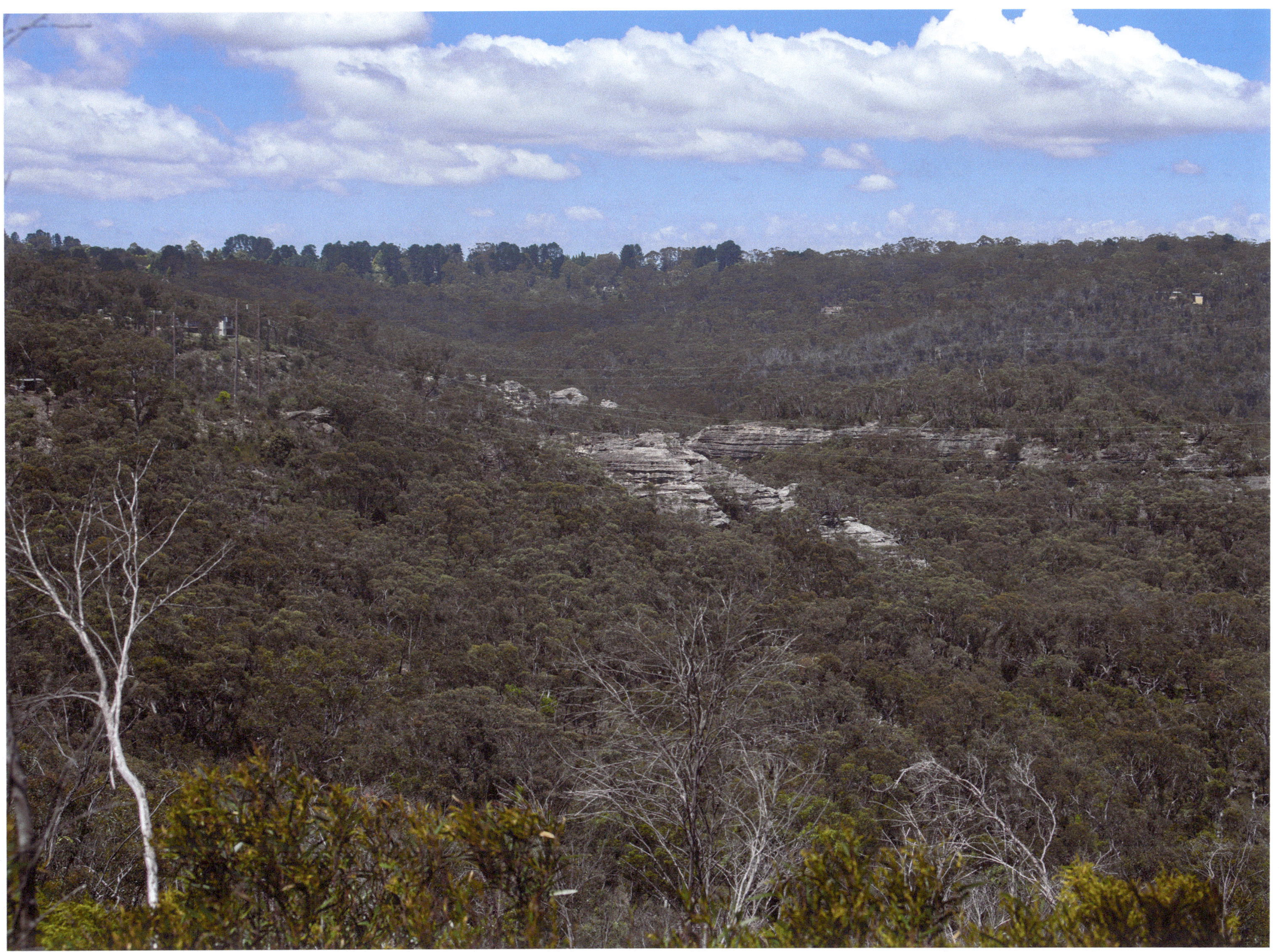

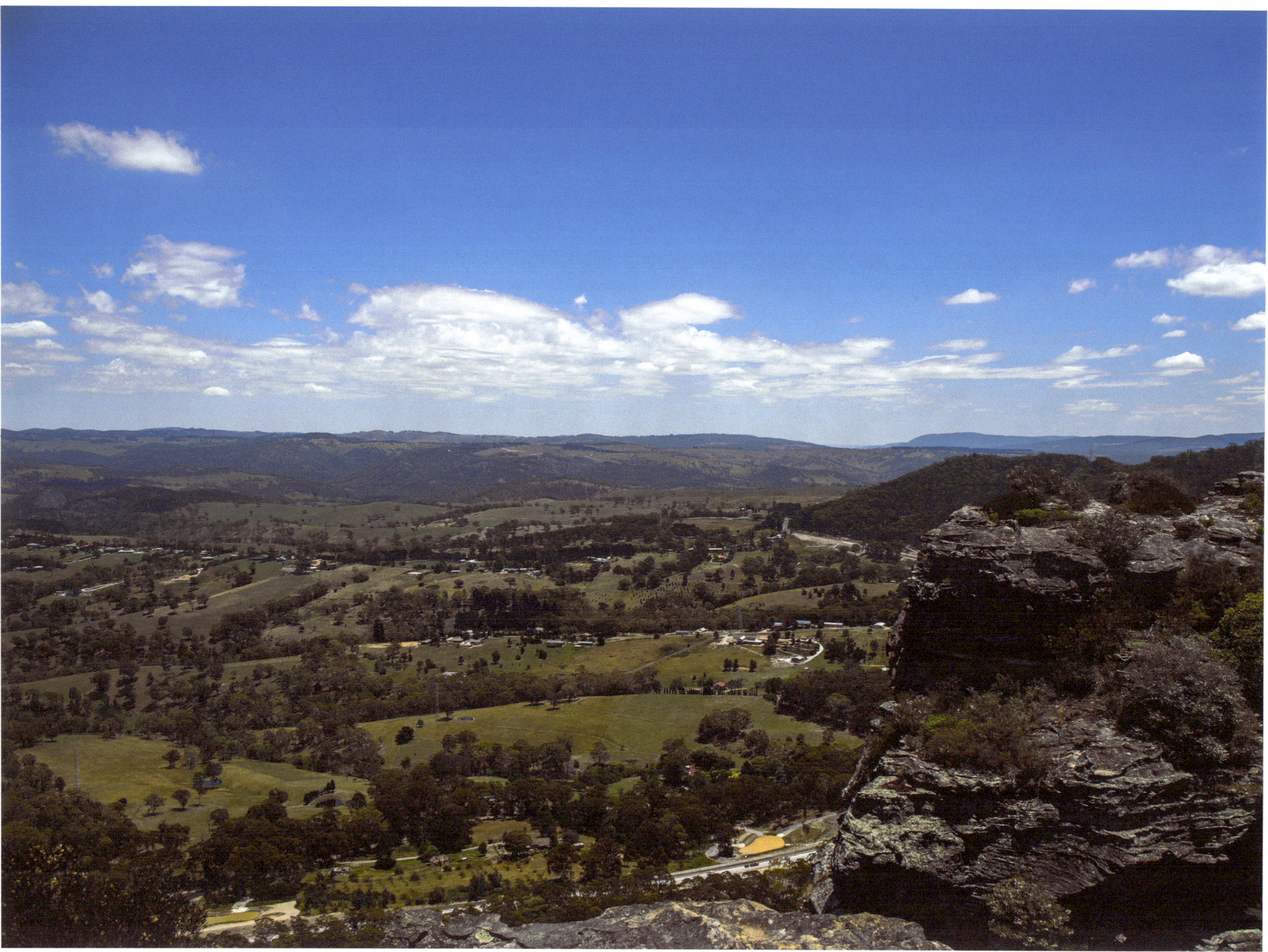

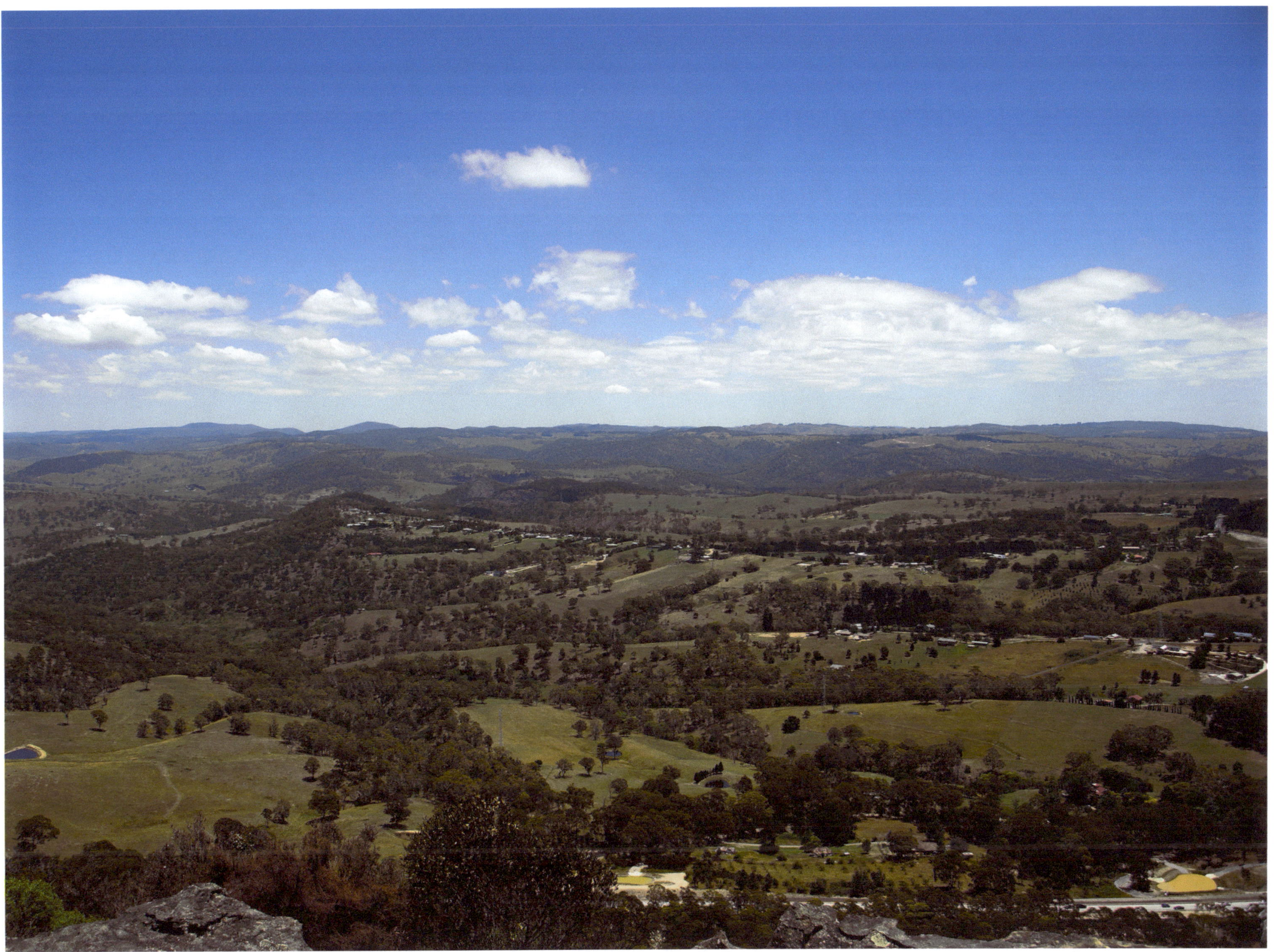

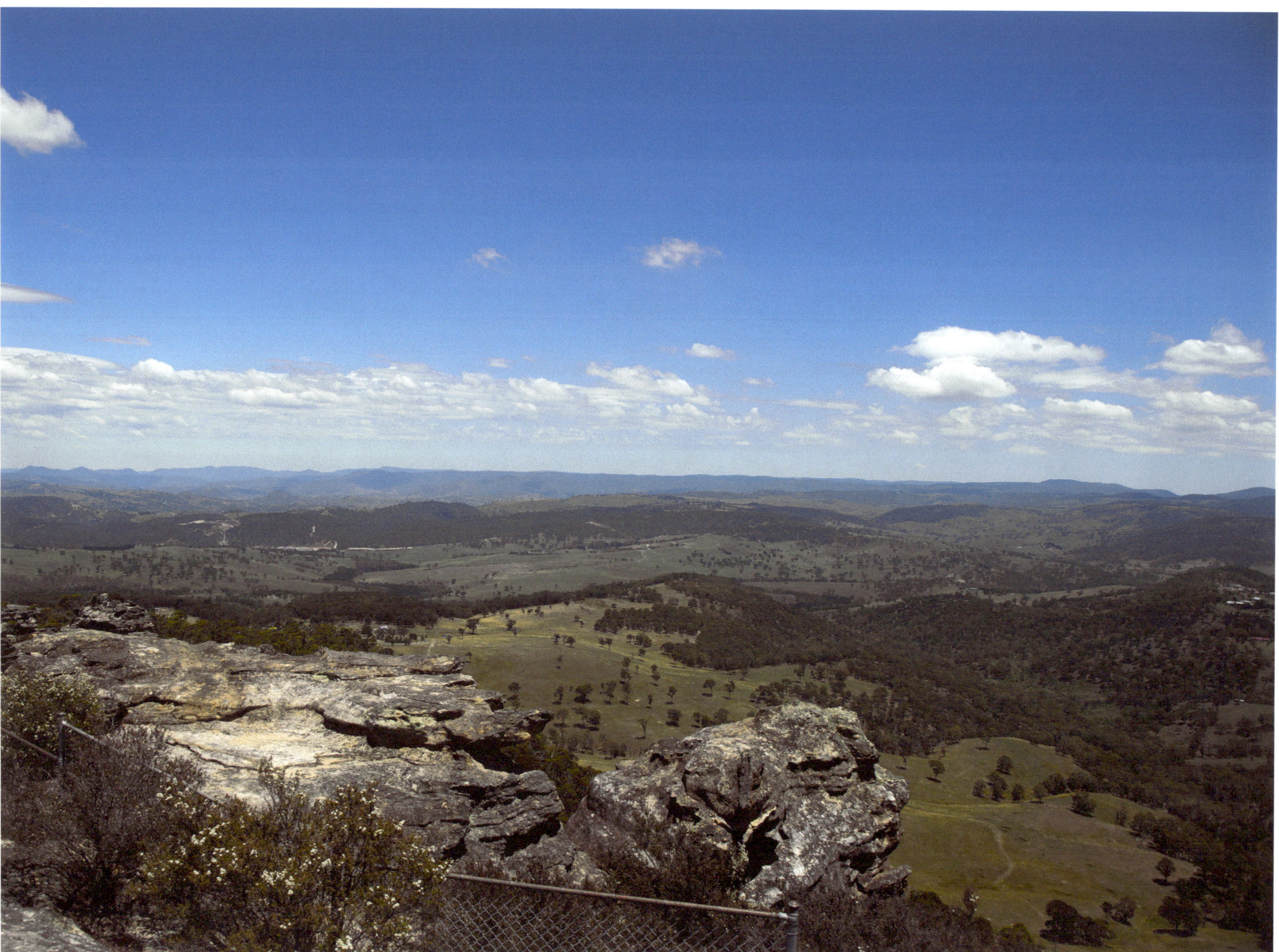

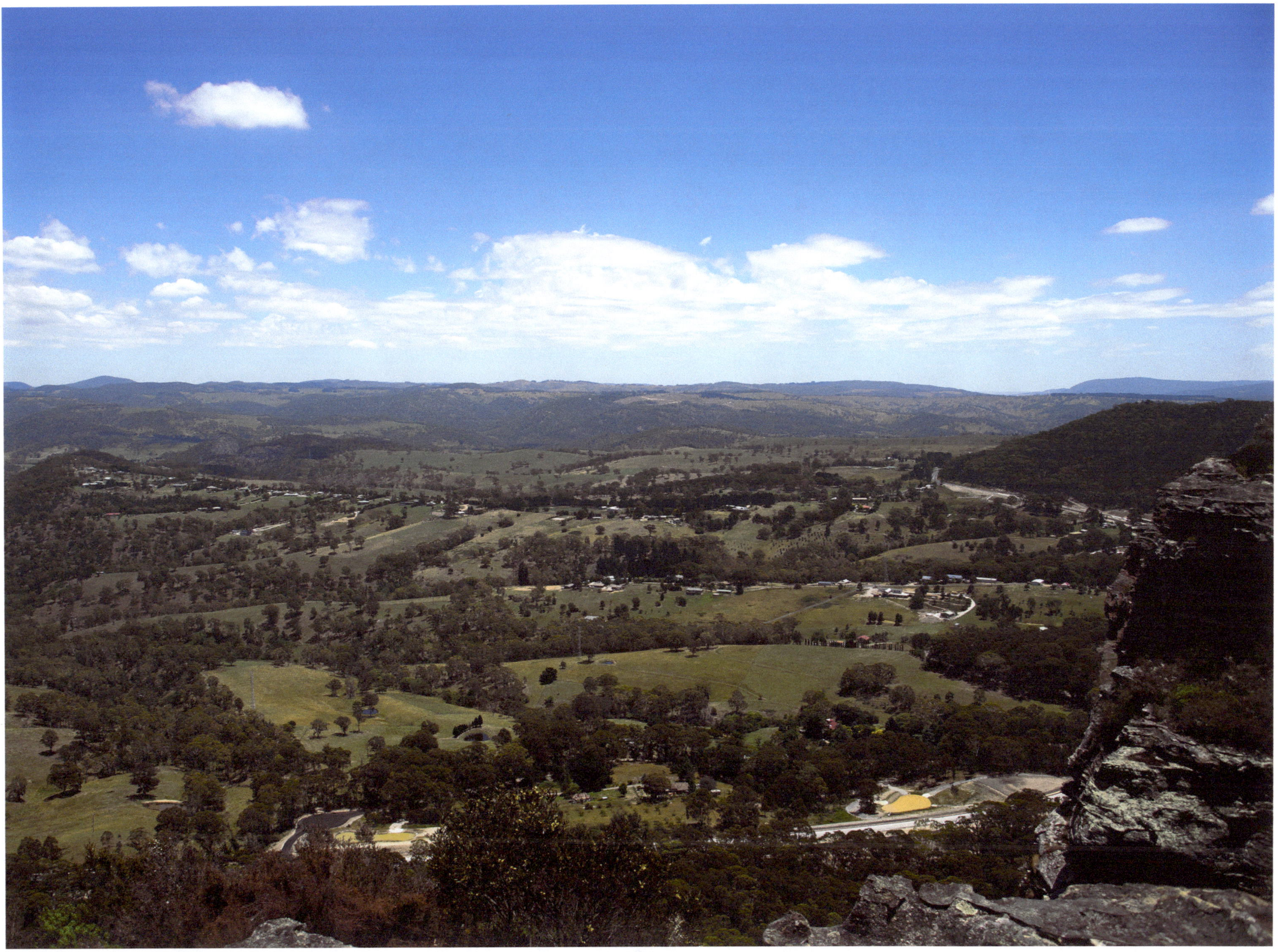

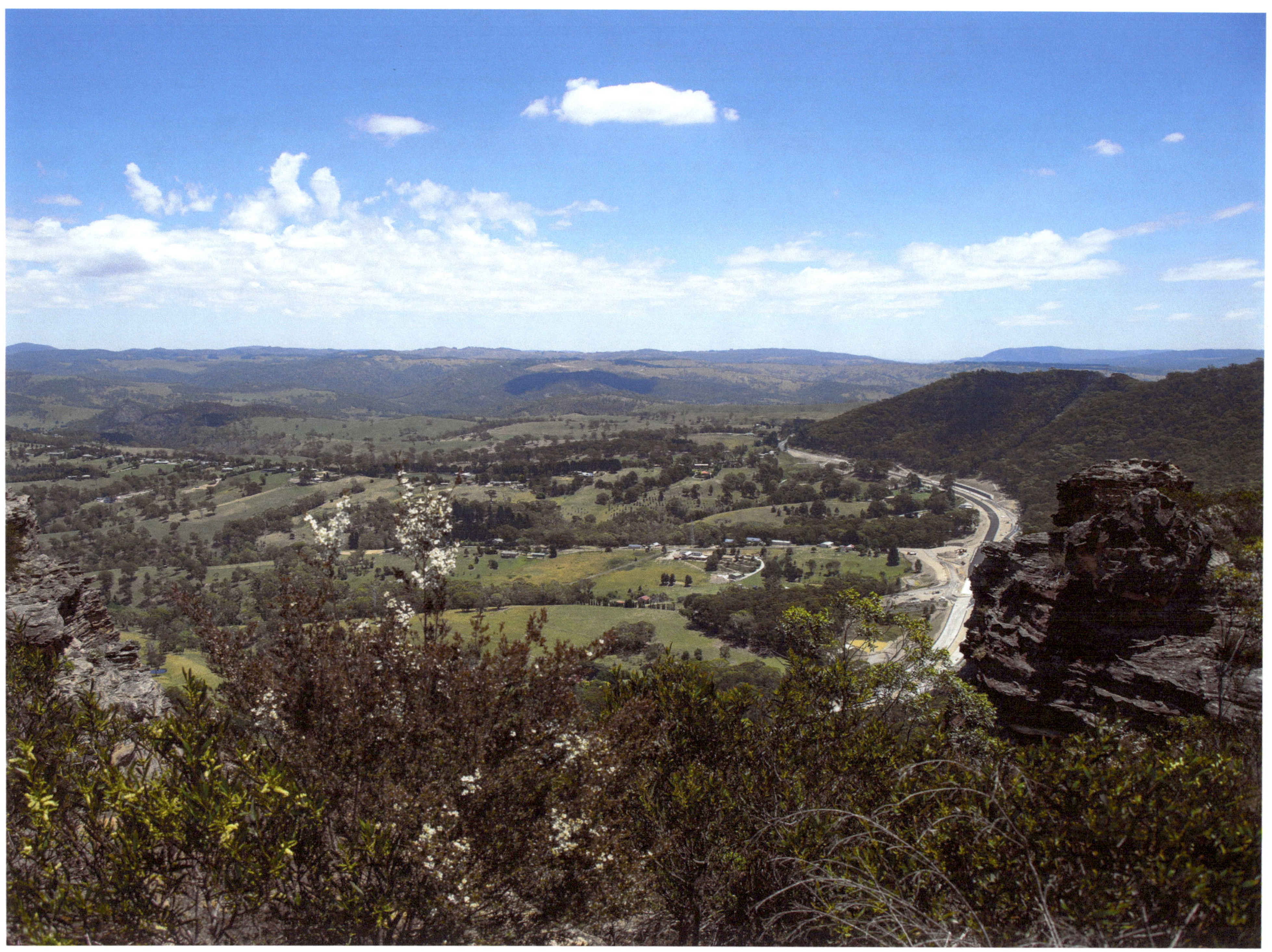

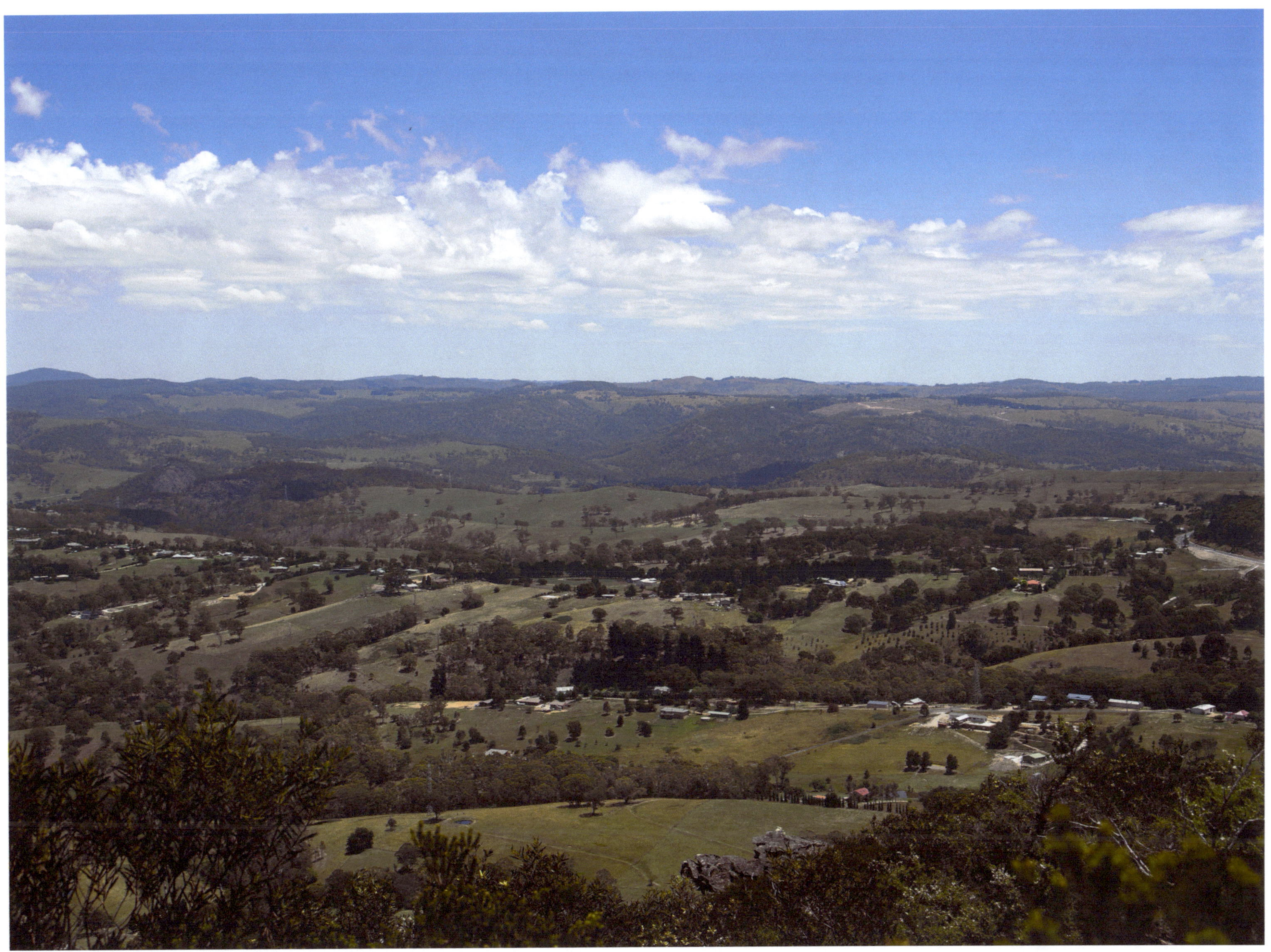

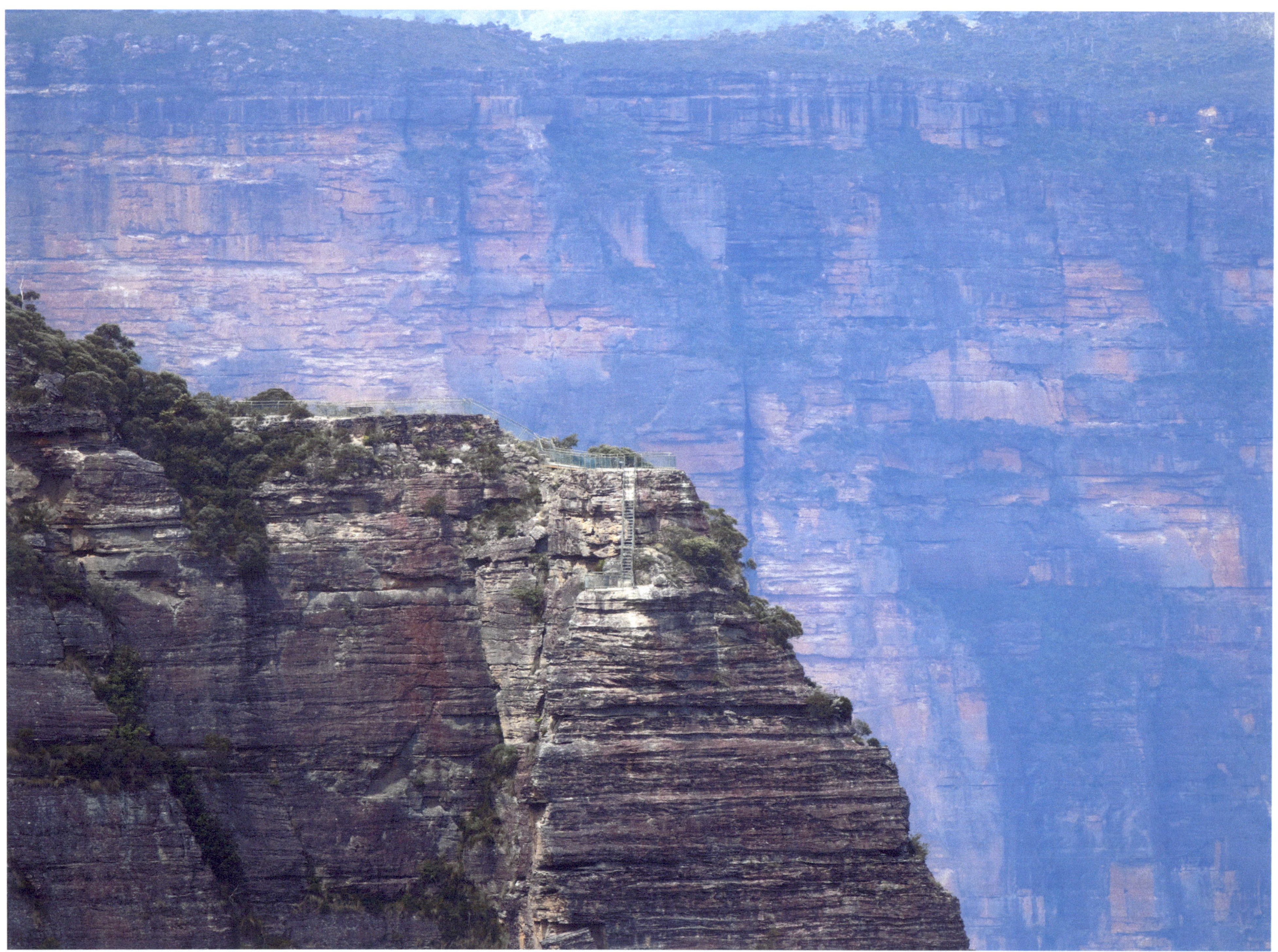

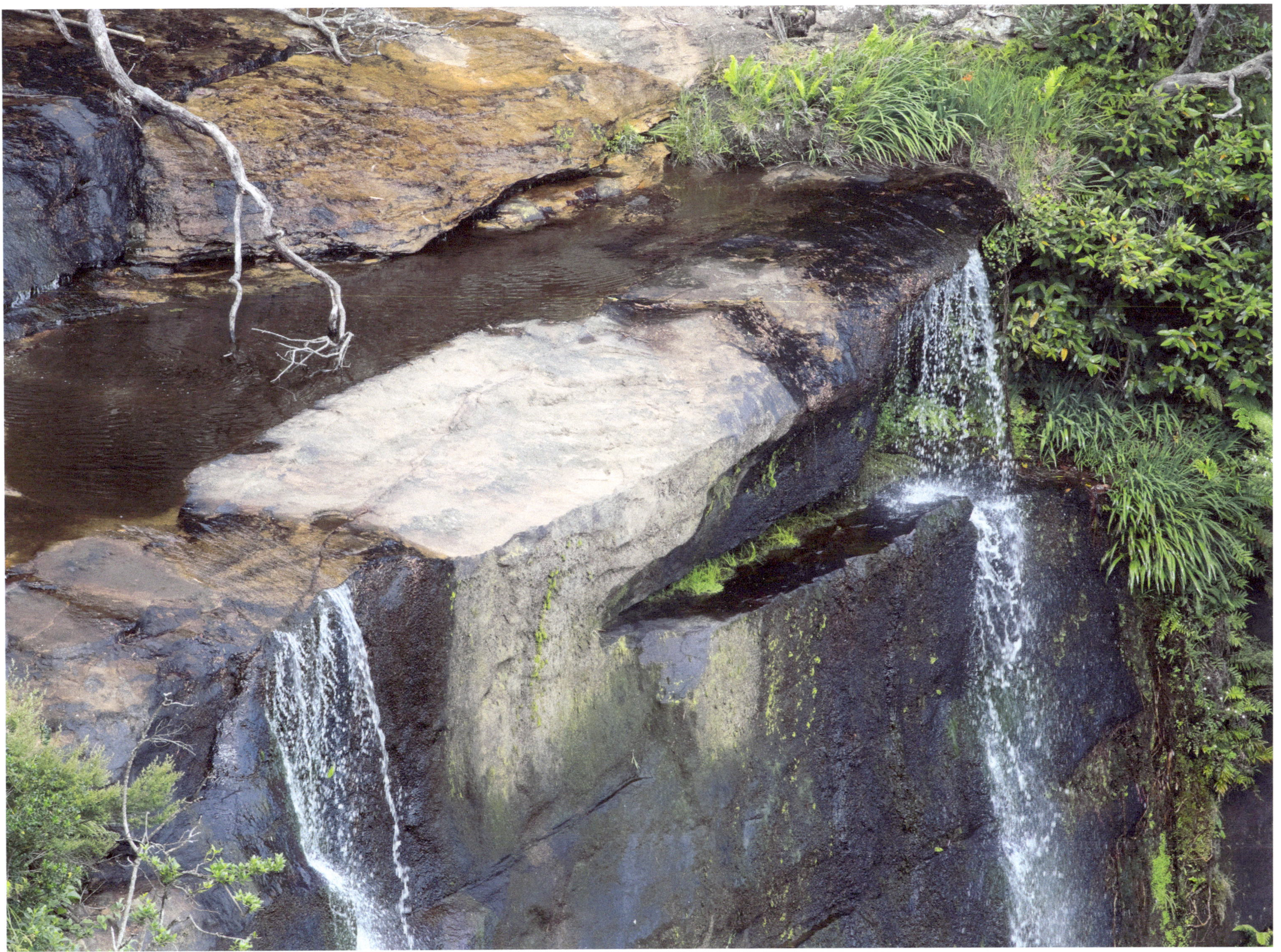

www.ingramcontent.com/pod-product-compliance
Lightning Source LLC
LaVergne TN
LVHW072331100826
845154LV00009B/152
* 9 7 8 0 9 9 8 0 6 8 2 6 8 *